Who **YOU** Are In Christ . . .
RIGHT NOW!

A Definitive Look at the **New Creation Realities**
That Have Become Established
Since the Resurrection of
the Lord Jesus Christ of Nazareth
From the Spiritual and Physical Dead

Robert E. Daley

The Larry Czerwonka Company, LLC
Hilo, Hawai'i

Copyright © 2016 by Robert E. Daley
All rights reserved.

No part of this publication may be reproduced, stored in or introduced into a retrieval system, or transmitted, in any form, or by any means (electronic, mechanical, photocopying, recording, or otherwise), without the prior permission of the publisher. Requests for permission should be directed to permissions@thelarryczerwonkacompany.com, or mailed to Permissions, The Larry Czerwonka Company, 1102 Apono Place, Hilo, Hawai'i 96720.

First Edition — June 2016

This book is set in 14-point Garamond

Published by: The Larry Czerwonka Company, LLC
czerwonkapublishing.com

Printed in the United States of America

ISBN: 0692725970
ISBN-13: 978-0692725979

Quantity Sales Discounts

Larry Czerwonka Company titles are available at significant quantity discounts when purchased in bulk for client gifts, sales promotions, and premiums. Special editions, including books with corporate logos, customized covers, and letters from the company or CEO printed in the front matter, as well as excerpts of existing books, can also be created in large quantities for special needs. For details and discount information contact: sales@thelarryczerwonkacompany.com

---

All scriptures used in this work are taken from the King James Version of the Scriptures.

BOOKS BY **ROBERT E. DALEY**

A Case for "Threes"
A Simple Plan . . . of Immense Complexity
Armour, Weapons, And Warfare
from Everlasting to Everlasting
Killer Sex
Life or Death, Heaven or Hell, You Choose!
Raptures and Resurrections
Short Tales
So . . . What Happens to the Package?
Study and Interpretation of The Scriptures Made Simple
Surviving Destruction as A Human Being
The Gospel of John
The Gospel of John (Red Edition)
The League of The Immortals
The New Testament - Pauline Revelation
The New Testament - Pauline Revelation Companion
"The World That Then Was . . ." & The Genesis That Now Is
What Color Are You?
What Makes A Christian Flaky?
What Really Happened to Judas Iscariot?
Who YOU Are in Christ . . . RIGHT NOW!

The Enhancement Series

#1 Book of Ecclesiastes
#2 Book of Daniel
#3 Book of Romans
#4 Book of Galatians
#5 Book of Hebrews

The Deeper Things of God Series

#1 The Personage of God
#2 The Personage of Man
#3 The Personage of Christ

Introduction

In detail, the *Pauline Revelation*, for the most part, declares the spiritual reality of who you are today in Christ, **RIGHT NOW**, and who you shall be in the Everlasting Millennia that lay ahead. **YOU** are a Human Being species of creation, which is . . .

Born-Again *(John 3:3, 5; I Peter 1:23)*,

Recreated *(Genesis 1:27; Psalms 102:18; Ephesians 1:10, 4:24)*,

Incorruptible *(I Corinthians 15:51-55)*,

Resurrected *(John 5:28-29; Romans 6:5)*,

Divinely Natured *(I Peter 1:4)*,

Chosen Before the Foundation of the World *(Ephesians 1:4)*,

Supernatural *(Matthew 17:20)*,

Redeemed *(Galatians 3:13)*,

Righteousness of God *(Ephesians 4:24)*,

More Than a Conqueror *(Romans 8:37)*,

Sin Free *(Ephesians 1:7)*,

Able to Do All Things *(Philippians 4:13),*
Predestinated *(Romans 8:29),*
Immortal *(I Timothy 1:10; I Corinthians 15:53),*
Christ-Minded *(I Corinthians 2:16),*
Chosen Generation *(I Peter 2:9),*
Eternally Indwelt and Empowered by the Holy Spirit *(John 14:16-17; Romans 8:11; I Corinthians 3:16; II Timothy 1:14),*
Blood-Related *(John 6:53-57; Ephesians 2:19; Hebrews 13:20-21),*
Complete in Him *(Colossians 2:10),*
Divine Heir *(Romans 8:17),*
Workmanship of God *(Ephesians 2:10),*
Royal Priesthood *(I Peter 2:9),*
Seated at the Right Hand *(Romans 8:34; Ephesians 1:20; Colossians 3:1; Hebrews 1:3),*
Administrative *(Revelation 22:5),*
Household Member *(Ephesians 2:19)*

. . . Of the Personal Family of the Most High God. And as such, 21st Century Christians should not be mealy-mouthed, limp-wristed, complacent, cowardly, doormat slaves to every lustful temptation of the flesh and of the mind, that the Devil would attempt to impose upon those who are woefully ignorant of who they are . . . not because of what they may have personally done, but rather, because of a lack of knowledge *(Hosea 4:6)* of what Christ Jesus our Superhero has accomplished.

New Testament spiritual realities have all been **Established by Faith** and shall be powerfully **Activated by Personal Belief.** Jesus of Nazareth brought forth these realities, and we need to receive and believe that they are ours.

It is time to rise up. It is time to learn who we really are. It is time to put aside the negativity and the denial, and embrace the truth. It is time for us to be the Men and Women of power and authority that our God has gone to great lengths to bring us unto. It is time!

Table of Contents

1. **Born-Again** . . . **1** *(John 3:3; 5; I Peter 1:23)*
2. **Recreated** . . . **8** *(Genesis 1:27; Psalms 102:18; Ephesians 1:10; 4:24)*
3. **Incorruptible** . . . **14** *(I Corinthians 15:51-55)*
4. **Resurrected** . . . **22** *(John 5:28-29; Romans 6:5)*
5. **Divinely Natured** . . . **27** *(I Peter 1:4)*
6. **Chosen From Before the Foundation of the World** . . . **33** *(Ephesians 1:4; Matthew 25:34; John 17:24)*
7. **Supernatural** . . . **38** *(Matthew 17:19-20)*
8. **Redeemed** . . . **42** *(Luke 1:67-70; Galatians 3:13-14; I Peter 1:18-21)*
9. **Righteousness of God** . . . **46** *(I Corinthians 1:30; Ephesians 4:24; II Corinthians 5:21)*
10. **More Than a Conqueror** . . . **51** *(Romans 8:37)*
11. **Sin Free** . . . **57** *(Romans 6:18; 22; 8:2; Ephesians 1:7)*
12. **Able To Do All Things** . . . **65** *(Philippians 4:13)*
13. **Predestinated** . . . **71** *(Romans 8:29)*
14. **Immortal** . . . **76** *(I Timothy 1:10; I Corinthians 15:53)*
15. **Christ-Minded** . . . **81** *(I Corinthians 2:16)*
16. **Chosen Generation** . . . **92** *(Matthew 1:17; I Peter 2:9; Romans 1:6; 8:28)*
17. **Eternally Indwelt and Empowered by the Holy Spirit** . . . **97** *(John 14:16-17; Rom. 8:11; I Corinth. 3:16)*
18. **Blood-Related** . . . **102** *(John 6:53-57; Ephesians 2:19; Hebrews 13:20-21)*
19. **Complete in Him** . . . **107** *(Colossians 2:10)*
20. **Divine Heir** . . . **112** *(Romans 8:17)*
21. **Workmanship of God** . . . **119** *(Ephesians 2:10)*
22. **Royal Priesthood** . . . **123** *(I Peter 2:9)*
23. **Seated at the Right Hand** . . . **132** *(Romans 8:34; Ephesians 1:20; Colossians 3:1; Hebrews 1:3)*
24. **Administrative** . . . **137** *(Revelation 22:3)*
25. **Household Member** . . . **142** *(Ephesians 2:19)*

BORN-AGAIN

CHAPTER 1

"Jesus answered and said unto him, Nicodemus, *verily, verily, I say unto thee, Except a man be* spiritually **Born-Again he cannot** perceive, or **see**, or in anywise understand **the Kingdom of God."** (John 3:3; Enhanced)

* * *

"Jesus answered, Verily, verily, I say unto thee, Except a man be physically **born of water** into this world, **and** then be born spiritually **of the** Holy **Spirit** of God, and pass from Spiritual Death unto Spiritual Life, **he cannot** legally **enter into the Kingdom of God."** (John 3:5; Enhanced)

The original Biblical terminology of **Born-Again**, as stated by Jesus of Nazareth in the verses above, has floated to the verbiage surface and become subject to deliberate misuse and abuse, specifically during the last forty years. Blasphemingly presenting, within a particular song, this spiritual reality as a lust-filled physical act or acquainting the New Birth with renewed physical or emotional vigor deliberately dilutes the seriousness of the spiritual reality necessity that was accom-

plished by Jesus of Nazareth upon his resurrection from both the spiritual and the physically dead.
(Colossians 1:15, 18; Hebrews 2:9, 14; Revelation 3:14)

"The Lord is not slack concerning his promise *of redemption,* ***as some men count slackness; but is long-suffering to us-ward, not willing that any*** *free-will moral creature* ***should perish, but that all should come to repentance."*** *(II Peter 3:9; Enhanced)*

God's love-affair with the Human race goes far beyond anything that has been emotionally expressed by men upon this planet Earth, concerning the subject of love. God is not without *feelings* and is not at all pleased when creations of love, given a free-will, choose to distance themselves from Him through disobedience and rebellion caused by Sin.

We are living in the End-of-Days, just before the prophetically declared Biblical Tribulation Period, and Satan has pulled out all of the stops in the raging warfare that actively exists on the Earth today. As children of Light, we must learn current spiritual realities and then align ourselves with the unchanging Word of God.

* * *

Unalterable Facts of Truth and Reality:

#1. The Personage of God is a Living Spirit Being. *(John 4:24)*

#2. Created creatures, known of as Human-Beings, were originally created **"in"** the image and **"after"** the likeness of the Personage of the Living God. *(Genesis 1:26)*

#3. Human-Beings were created Spiritually-Alive, and Soulishly-Alive, and Physically-Alive when God breathed into Adam's nostrils. *(Genesis 2:7)*

#4. Human-Beings were created 3-Dimensional in their construct, just like the Creator Himself... (A Spirit Dimension, and a Soul Dimension, and a Physical Dimension.)

#5. The Personage of Man was created to be a Living Spirit Human-Being. *(Genesis 2:17)*

#6. Within the locale known of as Heaven, where the Personage of God lives, only Living Spirit Beings are being allowed access and entrance. *(John 3:5)*

#7. Disobedience by the first Human-Being, named Adam, caused the Spirit Dimension of Adam to become acidically affected by the Law of Sin. The Life of God that was in him all leaked out, and his spirit became listless and without substance. The consequence was that Spiritual-Death occurred. *(Genesis 2:17)*

#8. That Spiritual-Death has been passed on down the road to every Human-Being through the process of Human-Being reproduction. *(Romans 5:12; Romans 3:23)*

#9. With the Spiritual-Death of Adam, the locale known of as Heaven became decidedly closed to all Spiritually-Dead Human-Beings. *(John 3:5)* No access or entrance is allowed.

#10. Original 3-Dimensional Human-Beings have now become 2-Dimensional Human-Beings when their Spirit Dimension died. *(Genesis 2:17; I Corinthians 2:14)*

#11. 2-Dimensional Human-Beings became Human-Beings that were Soulishly-Alive, and were Physically-Alive, but now are Spiritually-Dead. *(Genesis 2:7)*

#12. Every Human-Being coming forth after Adam's creation, that is born of a Human-Being father, has been physically born Spiritually-Dead.

#13. Within the locale known of as Heaven, where the Personage of God lives, Dead Spirit Beings, of any kind, are not being allowed access or entrance. *(John 3:5)*

Therefore:

A Human-Being... ALL HUMAN-BEINGS... must do what needs to be done to pass from Spiritual-Death back unto Spiritual-Life. They *must* become **Born-Again** within their Spirit-Dimension. The acidic holes of Sin must be repaired, *(II Corinthians 1:21-22; Ephesians 1:13; I John 3:9)* and their spirit needs to be filled with the Life of God once again, through the indwelling presence of the Holy Spirit. And that can only be accomplished by the power of the Holy Spirit of God, through surrender, and the placing of their trust in the finished work on the cross of the Lord Jesus Christ of Nazareth.

* * *

Spiritual Realities are not predicated upon the denominational preferences of Mankind. Spiritual Realities are not predicated upon any type of global religious insistence. Spiritual Realities are not predicated upon worldwide cultural traditions or customs. Spiritual Realities are predicated upon the Truth and only the Truth.

"Sanctify them *Father, and set them apart,* **through thy Truth: thy** *immutable* **word,** *the Scripture,* **is Truth."** *(John 17:17; Enhanced)*

The written Word of God, the Bible, is the bottom-line source of Truth and instruction concerning ***"all things that pertain unto life and godliness."*** *(II Peter 1:3)* Clarity of Spiritual Realities does not come from the Koran, or from the Book of Mormon, or from Sacred Scrolls, or Ancient Texts, or from Mystical Insights, or from any other postulated work that has emanated forth from the hand of men, and not come forth directly from God. *(II Peter 1:21)*

"Being** spiritually **Born-Again, not of corruptible seed, but of** that which is **incorruptible, by the Word of God, which liveth and abideth forever."
(I Peter 1:23; Enhanced)

It is an absolute necessity for a Human-Being to be spiritually **Born-Again** in order to have genuine spiritual insight and partake of Eternal Life from the Holy Spirit of God dwelling within them.

The Word of God is alive, and the Living Word of God, by the power of the Holy Spirit, is able to effect repair of the damage done by Sin to the spirit of any fallen Human-Being, and cause that a man or a woman becomes a partaker of Everlasting Life. *(II Corinthians 1:22; Ephesians 1:13, 4:30)*

If we are genuinely *in Christ,* then that Spiritual Reality has occurred. We are bubbling with the Life that Jesus came to this Earth to provide for men that have been previously separated from the love of God. May we revel in that truth and share the necessity of it with everyone that we meet.

* * *

Should we have surrendered to the accomplished finished work of Jesus Christ of Nazareth upon the cross of Calvary, then we are Born-Again within our own personal spirit, RIGHT NOW,

and are the Children of Light to a loving Heavenly Father, who is the Creator of all things.

All *New Creation Realities* are **<u>ESTABLISHED BY FAITH,</u>** *(The faith of Jesus of Nazareth)* *(John 1:12)* and those realities are personally **<u>ACTIVATED BY BELIEF!</u>** *(Of any particular individual Human Being) (John 6:29)*

RECREATED

CHAPTER 2

"So God created the Man in his own image, in the very image of God created he him, both male and female created he them." (Genesis 1:27; Enhanced)

* * *

"This shall be written for the fourteenth generation unto Christ to come, (Matthew 1:17) which is the Chosen Generation (I Peter 2:9): and the people which shall be Recreated shall praise the Lord." (Psalms 102:18; Enhanced)

* * *

"For we are his workmanship, Recreated in Christ Jesus unto good works, which God hath before the establishment of Time prophetically ordained that we should walk in them." (Ephesians 2:10; Enhanced)

* * *

"And that ye put on the New Creation man, which after the Personage of God Himself is Recreated in righteousness and true holiness." (Ephesians 4:24; Enhanced)

These select Scripture verses give unto us a brief synopsis of the Everlasting Plan that God has designed for the Hu-MAN-ity of Mankind... the Human-Being. And that plan is: To make a Created Creature to be as much like the Creator as is at all possible.

Now for us to understand these verses and ***"rightly divide the word of truth"*** *(II Timothy 2:15)* we must step way back and adopt a new perspective.

#1. God, as the Creator, is Immortal, and shall continue on within His existence capacity forever, and ever, and ever, and ever. This program that He has drafted for Mankind is not a *One-Hundred Years of Life on Earth, and We're Gone* program.

#2. Because of the Foreknowledge aspect of Omniscience *(Isaiah 46:10)* God is fully aware of the rebellion that shall occur amongst free-will moral beings that He intends to create.

#3. The created creature called MAN is not just another standard assembly-line product. This creature is patterned after the very Creator Himself. God intends on developing Himself an actual family, with whom He can share His creative treasures and endeavors.

#4. MAN is purposely created to be just like God on the inside, and to look just like the form *(Philippians 2.8)* and the shape *(John 5:37)* of God on the outside. *(Genesis 1:26)* The only things that will separate them from being <u>exactly</u> the same are what we call *The Non-Transferables* . . . the aspects of Omnipotence, Omniscience, Omnipresence, and Self-Existence from Everlasting.

#5. The first prototype named Adam is brought forth, and during the testing portion of the program, he sadly fails. The Creator must work with what is viably left of the original creation, and the process of bringing us to the threshold of a second, and last, *New Creation* takes approximately four-thousand years of operational *Time*.

#6. The second prototype becomes a New Species of Human-Being creation upon his resurrection from the dead. All of the prophetical declarations that have ever been uttered for this very purpose are brought together. They are collectively mixed and interwoven with a Human body of Sinless-flesh that lies silently within a dank sepulcher. And under the rules and regulations of a newly established Law *(Romans 8:2)* a brand-new, New Creation is creatively brought forth.

#7. This New Creation is unprecedented. This New Creation is not simply a remodel of the old original. This New Creation is the realized finished product of Divine desire and design. This New Creation is of a Ruling Class. This New Creation is a limited edition . . . a two-thousand-year window of invitation and opportunity is all that shall be afforded for this elite project.

* * *

When God first created MAN, He knew the depth of what He was dealing with and bringing forth. He knew that in a relatively few short centuries, He also would be putting on an altered reproduction of the Terrestrial Body that He had originally created for the MAN to live in. *(Psalms 40:6-8; Hebrews 10:5)* When that event actually occurred you now have the living Personage of God walking around upon this Earth in an altered Terrestrial Body *Earth-Suit* . . . and planning to use that body, and the dimension of the soul, as a viable sacrifice in completing the payment of debt that the Law of Sin had demanded from MAN when Adam fell and became a subject to whom he obeyed. *(Romans 6:16; I Timothy 2:14)*

Jesus of Nazareth is a real Human-Being person who has been made **"like unto his brethren"** in every respect. *(Hebrews 2:17)* He is fully a MAN and is always doing those things that are pleasing unto his God. *(John 8:29)* He is here to fulfill Covenant promises and to pay an exorbitant price for heinousness which he did not personally owe.

When the hour came, he submitted himself unto the unspeakable torture and death of the cross and suffered a tremendous loss. His Spirit-Dimension *(II Corinthians 5:21)* and his Body-Dimension *(Hebrews 9:26)* were offered in a sacrificial manner to fulfill needed payment for willfully errant intellectual and emotional activities, and the ill-health and all physical deficits that pertain to the original Terrestrial Body design that has been tainted and affected by Sin.

Divine *Light* *(I John 1:5)* was snuffed out like a candle because of the Darkness caused by Sin. Divine *Life* was swallowed-up by the Death-null of the Law of Sin. *(Romans 6:23)* But Divine *Love* *(I John 4:8)* was not able to be affected or even touched by either the Darkness or the Death. Divine *Love* reigned triumphant... carrying our precious Savior from one *testator* *(Hebrews 9:16)* side of the cross to the other *testator* *(Hebrews 1:2)* side of the cross... and *New Spirit Life* and Terrestrial Bodily resurrection was made possible because Divine *Love* is a love that **"never fails."** *(I Corinthians 13:8)*

An original Creation had occurred four-thousand years before a needed resurrection. The initial ingredients of that original Creation have since all been used up. A *Re*creation is the only possible option that is available, using the residue of the original Creation ingredients that could be salvaged from the Law of Sin's grasp.

* * *

We are related to a MAN named Adam by reason of Human-Being reproduction. However, we are a *Recreated* Human-Being *in Christ* RIGHT NOW! A Human-Being species, of a *New Creation*,

because of what Jesus of Nazareth has accomplished. Newly alive, and victorious, and Brand-New because of Christ. _**ESTABLISHED BY FAITH**_ and personally _**ACTIVATED BY BELIEF**_.

INCORRUPTIBLE

CHAPTER 3

"Behold, I show you a revelation *mystery; we shall not all sleep in* Physical Death, *but we shall all be changed.*

In a moment, in the twinkling of an eye, at the sound of the *last trump*et: *for the trumpet shall sound, and the* Physically *Dead shall be raised incorruptible, and we* which are alive and remain *shall be changed.*

For this corruptible flesh *must put on Incorruption, and this mortal* condition *must put on Immortality.*

So when this corruptible flesh *shall have put on Incorruption, and this mortal* condition *shall have put on Immortality, then shall be brought to pass the saying that is written* by Isaiah the prophet, *Death is swallowed up in victory.* (Isaiah 25:8)

O Death, where is thy sting? O grave, where is thy victory?" (I Corinthians 15:51-55; Enhanced)

Along with its sister statement found within the Book of I Thessalonians, chapter 4, verses 16 and 17, one could not find a more encouraging declaration of the promise made by the Holy Spirit of Grace.

Just think of it... from a sin affected, diseased, deteriorating, growing-old, weakening natural Terrestrial Body, to a sin free, completely well and whole, ever strong and constant, never aging, sustained, supernatural, Spiritual Body. *(I Corinthians 15:44)*

*** Special Notation:** *The Body of Christ is quite a unique entity as a whole. It is indeed a single organism, but it is made up of various parts. (Ephesians 4:4) And God even uses the natural Terrestrial Body of a Man to illustrate the operation of what the finished work of Christ has really established. One of the difficulties that we have today, is that we do not make the jump to light-speed, and really grasp hold of what is currently flailing around us in its fledgling years of operation RIGHT NOW, and understand what the future will manifest in its fullness when men finally renew their minds and harmonize with what God is going to be working with throughout all of Eternity.*

What Jewish Jesus of Nazareth accomplished he effected for the benefit of all of Mankind. Sadly, all of Mankind will not look beyond their race, religion, creed or customs, and readily accept it. Most of the people within this sin-saturated world will ignorantly reject the creative God of Love, unwittingly choosing, the tormenting fire of pain and separation. Spiritual truths do not change just because people are unaware of them. The Gospel is imperative! The Word of God must go forth!

* * *

Currently, corruption surrounds us and continually pummels us with natural reminders, using all things familiar. The unchangeable Scripture, however, paints a different picture of reality. So . . . whose report will we believe?

It is true that we live in a corruptible, sin-saturated, world of physical sickness and disease. But the Word of God prophetically declared.

"Surely he hath borne our griefs, and carried our sorrows: yet we did esteem him stricken, smitten and tormented **of God, and afflicted.**

But he was actually **wounded for our transgressions,** and **he was** personally **bruised for our iniquities: the chastisement of our peace was** laid **upon him, and with his** scourging **stripes we are** totally, physically **healed** even Right Now." (Isaiah 53:4-5; Enhanced)

Even within the New Testament it is confirmed that,

"Who his own self bare our sins in his own body on the tree, so **that we, being dead to sins,**

should live unto righteousness: by whose *scourging* ***stripes ye were*** *totally, physically* ***healed*** *even Right Now."* (I Peter 2:24; Enhanced)

The two major, visible and pronounced areas of Christian victory for those who are *in Christ* are finances and physical healing. The whole world is watching to see how we, as children of the Most High God, are going to handle these sensitive issues. Finances are tied directly, by Scriptural mandate, to tithing . . . but we will save that one for another time.

Physical healing is a finished reality of the Right Now. Physical sickness or disease speaks of corruption . . . the natural Terrestrial Body operating according to the Natural Laws that govern this planet because of Sin. The Scriptures declare the reality of Incorruption . . . according to the finished work of Jesus of Nazareth, and the Spiritual Laws that govern resurrection realities. So which will it be? There is not another work to be found within the Scriptural account that reveals something else that God is going to do so that we might be free from the bondage and frustration of physical sickness and disease. There is no planned future work.

It is high time for us to wake-up to the Spiritual Truth of Scripture, learn who we are *in Christ*, become knowledgeable of the **"weapons of our warfare,"**

(II Corinthians 10:4) begin to exercise our authority, **"*speaking things that be not as though they were,*"** *(Romans 4:17)* and enjoy the victory that Jesus won for us. You ... do not have to be physically sick another day for the rest of your entire life!

It is not as though the Devil is not going to attack you anymore. It is not as though the Devil is going to freely acknowledge Jesus' victory that he obtained at the cross. It is not as though the Devil is simply going to *allow* you to Cadillac right along. We are in a real-live warfare ... but not against other Human-Beings. Get your Bible. Open up to the promises or realities of a God, who does not lie. Insistently declare with your mouth what the Word of God clearly states. Take your stand as a victorious child of God. Do not allow yourself to be persuaded by what the doctor tells you. Do not allow yourself to be persuaded by what your body will tell you. Do not allow yourself to be persuaded by what your friends or your family say to you. Stand on what God tells you! Declare with your mouth, over and over and over again, the spiritual reality of Truth! You are healed ... ! you are not <u>going</u> to be healed ... you <u>are</u> healed RIGHT NOW! Memorize the Scriptures on healing! Get them into your mind ... and then work them continually until they drop down into your heart! Remember ... **Established by Faith,** but personally **Activated by Belief!**

If you think that ***believing*** is easy, then you are truly mistaken. ***Believing*** belongs to the Realm of the Spirit . . . and you are living within the Realm of the Natural. Everything around you is going to shout at you *Natural, Natural, Natural.* The reason that the Word of God tells us to **"*renew your mind*"** *(Romans 12:2; Ephesians 4:23)* is to clearly point the way into the Realm of the Spirit.

* ***Special Notation:*** *If you change what a Man thinks within his mind (Proverbs 23:7) . . . you will automatically change what the Man comes to believe in his heart. If you change what a Man believes within his heart (Mark 11:24) . . . you will automatically change the words that come out of the Man's mouth. If you change the words that come out of a Man's mouth (Mark 11:23; Romans 4:17) . . . you will automatically change what the Man receives into his hands. (Mark 11:24)*

But, it all starts with the mind. It all starts with the Control Center of the Person. It all starts within the Corporate ***Head-***quarters. We have already been *Programmed by Life's Natural Experiences* from the time that we were born. What we currently think . . . yea, what we currently ***believe*** at the present, is the total accumulation of *Mom and Dad, Friends and Family, Teachers and Ministers, Professionals and Non-Professionals, Television and Movies, Books and Periodicals,* and various accumulated information that has been presented to us from innumerable other sources.

When we stack all of that up against what the Holy Scriptures declare... whose report will we believe? *(Isaiah 53:1; Romans 10:16)* With the limp-wristed, mediocre approach that is normally taken with things of a spiritual nature, we definitely have a lot of work to do!

The fact of the matter is that Scriptural New Creation Realities declare that we are resident within the finished work of the cross RIGHT NOW... which includes INCORRUPTION. The Natural will say... it's not yours yet... it's still in the future, can't you read the tense of the verse? The Natural also said that Jairus' daughter was dead—but Jesus, the living Word of God, said that she was sleeping! Whose report would you like to believe? Would you rather walk in Corruption or Incorruption? You choose!

* * *

Because of Jesus' sacrificial work upon the cross of Calvary, and subsequent Resurrection from the spiritual and physical dead, we are partakers of the New Creation Spiritual Realities and Promises. These promises are actually for the RIGHT NOW as well as for the eons ahead!

They have already all been *<u>ESTABLISHED BY FAITH</u>* and await a personal *ACTIVATION*

BY BELIEF. So . . . what would you like to do . . . the choice is yours?

RESURRECTED

CHAPTER 4

"That I may know him more intimately, and grasp an understanding of the power of his resurrection, and become a partaker of the fellowship of his sufferings, actually being made conformable unto his death;

If by any means I too might attain unto the resurrection of the dead." *(Philippians 3:10-11; Enhanced)*

The desperate cry of the Apostle Paul's heart needs to become the desiring cry of our heart as well. The *New Birth* gives unto us an entrance into an exciting new Supernatural Realm of existence and operation. We have never ever been here before this hour. Up until now we have been prisoners of the Natural World and the functions and activities of only that which can be seen, or heard, or smelled, or tasted, or touched. We have been Spiritually-Dead in our sins and assigned unto condemnation when life on this Earth is over. *(John 3:18-21)*

But because of Christ Jesus, and what he has done for us, we are now New Creatures. Hallelujah! We have a brand-new life! We have been adopted by God! And an understanding of *"the power of his resurrection"* goes so much further than simply the reality of a dead man being raised back-up unto physical life again.

His Super-Nova detonation, impacting resurrection, has changed everything. Time calculation has been affected by that resurrection. The Realm that we know of as Heaven has been re-opened to accommodate living spirit beings. The kingdom of darkness operating on this Earth has been stopped in its tracks and its activities subject to suspension. Effective prayer has been augmented. Real power has been once again placed within the hands of those that it belongs to. Authority is no longer subject to the override of Sin's influence. And children of the Most High God are now set into the driver's seat for future visionary fulfillment. Fasten your seat belts!

We now revel in the **"fellowship of his sufferings"** so that our identification with what he has provided will not just ring true for us, but that the explosion of that which was accomplished for the whole of Humanity will resonate within our hearts. Jesus **"suffered"** being tempted . . . and we need to remain mindful of that when *Hell* throws something our way to derail us from our present course. We also should **"submit ourselves therefore to God"** and **"resist the devil"** and watch him flee. *(James 4:7)* Jesus **"suffered"** a contradiction of sinners against himself, being a man of love in a world of hate; a man of truth in a world of lies; and a man of mercy and forgiveness in a world of an *eye-for-an-eye*. We should do no less.

Jesus became Sin, *(II Corinthians 5:21)* and died to destroy Sin, and the one who had the power of death through Sin. *(Hebrews 2:14)* We must **"lay aside every weight, and the sin which doth so easily beset us"** and walk in the New Life that we have been given as Children of Light. We can no longer vacillate between what we know is right and that which we *feel* so pressured to want to engage in. The strength is to be found *in Christ*. *(Philippians 2:13)*

"Marvel not at this. For the hour is coming, in the which all that are in the graves shall hear his voice,

And shall come forth. They that are Born-Again, and **have done good, unto the Resurrection of Life** Everlasting . . . **and they that** are not begotten from above, and **have done evil, unto the Resurrection of Damnation** forevermore." *(John 5:28-29; Enhanced)*

Jesus prophetically spoke about the *after death* condition, and the reality that awaits all Human-Beings. At the time of this declaration, the *New Birth* was not yet a reality because Jesus is **"the first begotten of the dead,"** *(Revelation 1:5)* and while he is talking to Nicodemus, he is not yet crucified and then raised up.

There are Scripturally five separate *events* that make up the First Resurrection unto Everlasting Life. *(Revelation 20:5)* The Resurrection of Jesus of Nazareth is the first event, *(Revelation 1:5)* . . . the Saints that Slept is the second event, *(Matthew 27:52-53)* . . . the Dead in Christ is the third event, *(I Thessalonians 4:16)* . . . the Tribulation Martyrs are the fourth event, *(Revelation 6:9-11; 7:13-14; 20:4)* . . . and the Two Witnesses named Enoch and Elijah are the fifth event. *(Revelation 11:7-12; 20:5)*

Resurrection from the dead is actually the antidote to the incurable disease of Physical Death. And during this current Probationary Period of Mankind **"as it is appointed unto** *all* **men once to** *physically* **die, but after this the judgment,"** if one finds themselves *in Christ*, there is a precious promise from a faithful Savior. *(Hebrews 9:27)*

"For the Lord himself shall descend from the **Heaven with a shout, with the voice of the Archangel** Michael**, and with the trumpet of God: and the** *physically* **dead in Christ shall rise first.**

<u>**Then we which are** *physically* **alive and remain shall be caught up together with them in the clouds,**</u> **to meet the Lord in the air: and so shall we ever be with the Lord."** *(I Thessalonians 4:16-17; Enhanced)*

We have already met the legal requirements of Physical Resurrection by our identification with Christ Jesus, and are privileged, within this generation, to by-pass the actuality of bodily cessation of life's necessities, and to be *"caught up together with them"* and *"be changed,*

In a moment, in the twinkling of an eye, at the last trumpet. For the trumpet shall sound, and the physically *dead* in Christ *shall be raised incorruptible, and we* that are spiritually Born-Again *shall be changed.* (I Thessalonians 4:17; I Corinthians 15:51-52; Enhanced)

* * *

"For if we have been planted together in the likeness of his death, we shall be also likewise raised up unto New Life *in the likeness of his resurrection."* (Romans 6:5; Enhanced)

* * *

Because we find ourselves *in Christ* **RIGHT NOW**, we are already resurrected by faith, within the finished work of Jesus of Nazareth upon the hill of Calvary . . . and we are anticipatingly biding our time.

<u>**ESTABLISHED BY FAITH**</u> and now personally <u>***ACTIVATED BY BELIEF***</u> once again!

DIVINELY NATURED

CHAPTER 5

Nature—*as defined by Webster's Ninth New Collegiate Dictionary.*

1.) a. *the inherent character or basic constitution of a person or thing:* ESSENCE

2.) a. *a creative and controlling force in the universe* **b.** *an inner force or the sum of such forces in an individual*

3.) *a kind or class usually distinguished by fundamental or essential characteristics*

4.) *the physical constitution or drives of an organism*

7.) a. *man's original or natural condition*

"Whereby are given unto us exceeding great and precious promises: that by these *promises* **ye might become partakers of the Divine nature** *of God,* **having escaped the corruption that is** *running rampant* **in the world through lust."** *(II Peter 1:4; Enhanced)*

The *Nature* of something or of someone is the summation of the totality of what constitutes their entire being. The *Nature* of God is concisely stated within I Corinthians 13 . . .

"*Agape Love* **suffereth long, and is** *extremely* **kind.** *Agape Love* **envieth not** *anyone nor anything.* *Agape Love* **vaunteth not itself,** *and* **is not puffed up.**

Agape Love **doth not behave itself unseemly,** *and* **seeketh not her own** *way,* *and* **is not easily provoked,** *and* **thinketh no evil.**

Agape Love **rejoiceth not in iniquity, but rejoiceth** *always* **in the truth.**

Agape Love **beareth all things,** *and* **believeth all things,** *and* **hopeth all things,** *and* **endureth all things.**

Agape Love **never faileth."** *(I Corinthians 13:4-8a; Enhanced)*

This is a description, from the Spirit of Truth himself, of the Personage of God's *Nature*. This is a description of the Personage of God's character. This sums up the totality of the *ESSENSE* of the Personage of God.

* * *

All free-will, intelligent, moral, created creatures also have *Natures* which reveals to us the *Essence* of their particular being.

The being that we would have the least amount of information about Scripturally is referred to as *Other Creatures. (Romans 8:39)* These were the first inhabitants of the planet Earth. They were the fledgling society that was in need of governance and became placed under the oversight of a Holy Angel in training. *(Isaiah 14:13; Ezekiel 28:15)* When the Holy Angel turned against God, they followed him in his pursuit of power. Judgment resulted in the drowning of their Terrestrial Bodies *(Psalms 104:6)* and they became the disembodied spirit beings that today we know of as Demons. [*Earth is not the only planet within this Universe that was, and is, populated with Other Creatures. However, within the Scriptures they are known of as Thrones or Dominions or Principalities or Powers. (Colossians 1:16)*] We know very little about their *Nature*, and are only able to deduce that they are free-willed *(otherwise they would not be able to turn against God)*, and that they are moral *(otherwise they would not be held accountable for their bad decisions)*, and that they are intelligent *(otherwise the demons that Jesus of Nazareth encountered would not speak to him and attempt to bargain with him the way that they did)*, and that we have no Scriptural record whatsoever of them being given the gift of reproductive permission. Whatever their original *Nature* was like, it became defiled and tainted because of the power of the Law of Sin, and the only residue of insight that we have is of an *Other Creature/Satanic Nature* that we find connected with Demons.

The next Creation Category of being that we would know about is *Angels—Holy and Unholy*. *Holy Angels* would be free-willed *(otherwise they could not turn against God and become Unholy Angels)*, and they are moral *(otherwise the Unholy Angels would not be held accountable for the bad decisions that they have made)*, and they are intelligent *(as is testified of within the various Scriptural events and dealings that have taken place between Holy Angels and God, and between Holy Angels and Man)*, and we have no Scriptural record whatsoever of *Holy Angels* being given reproductive permission either. *(Mainly, because there is no Scriptural record of there being any female Holy Angels.)* The *Nature* of *Holy Angels* remains clean and pure. Their *Nature* is not the same as the *Nature* of men, or as the *Nature* of God. They are an exalted species of creation that have been created for the purpose of willful servitude, to both God and Man. However, that servitude is not one of compulsion but rather one of desire. *Holy Angels* that have become *Unholy Angels* have had their *Natures* altered and defiled by the power of the Law of Sin. Their *Nature* would no longer be a pure *Angelic Nature* but rather has become an *Angelic/Sin Nature*.

And lastly, when *MAN* was created he had a completely *Human Nature*. But the entrance and operation of Sin changed all of that as it did with the first two Creation Categories of creatures. Because he was a unique created creature within his own right his *Nature* belonged only to him, and was not *shareable*. * Jesus Christ of Nazareth is the Personage of God . . . who became a Man. This God/Man ministered upon the planet and was captured by God's archenemy, an *Unholy Angel*, and put to death. This God/Man did not stay dead, but was *Re*-created concerning his Humanity, and was physically raised up to life again. He was still God, but his death afforded the Godhead an opportunity to bring forth a brand New Species of Human Being creation that is, within the days in which we live, only two-thousand years old. An extremely short invitation, time wise, has been extended by God for any fallen Human Being that would like to identify with Christ Jesus, and put their trust in what he did . . . and believe that he actually did it for them. Should that reality be chosen, they would literally become a part of Christ Jesus *(Ephesians 5:30)* and realize a change in their very *Nature*. They would no longer possess a *Human Being/Satanic Nature*, but would instead experience a new *Human Being/Divine Nature*. They would become the ideal God-like creation that the Almighty Creator intended Man to be in the first place. They would become just like God, only without Omniscience, Omnipotence, Omnipresence, and Self-Existence from Everlasting. They would, in reality, become the small g . . . children of the big G . . . Father of all of creation. *(Psalms 82:6; John 10:34-35)*

* * *

Divine Nature has been lovingly extended by God unto those creations of the Human-Being species that have surrendered to love and mercy and grace. That Nature is certainly able to be enjoyed **RIGHT NOW,** but most assuredly shall become permanent for those individuals who pursue righteousness and holiness and who do not *fall away.* *(Hebrews 6:4-6)*

<u>ESTABLISHED BY FAITH</u> and personally realized with ***<u>ACTIVATION BY BELIEF.</u>***

CHOSEN BEFORE THE FOUNDATION OF THE WORLD

CHAPTER 6

"According as he hath specifically chosen us to be in him before the foundation of the world was even laid, that we should be holy and without blame before him in love." (Ephesians 1:4; Enhanced)

* * *

"Then shall the King of the Kingdom of Heaven say unto them on his right hand, Come, ye blessed of my Father, inherit the kingdom which was prepared for you from the foundation of the world." (Matthew 25:34; Enhanced)

* * *

"Father, I will that they also, whom thou hast given unto me, may be with me where I am. That they may behold my glory which thou hast given unto me. For thou lovedst me even before the foundation of the world." (John 17:24; Enhanced)

The work of God that we are a part of RIGHT NOW is a work of *Predestination.* It is the only genuine work of *Predestination* that we have a Scriptural record of. What causes this work to be a genuine work of *Predestination* is the fact that the entire project has been accomplished solely by the Three Members of the Godhead, who never vary in Their own exercise of *Free-Will*.

*"**Declaring the end** of a work **from the** very **beginning. And from ancient times the things that are not yet done, saying, My counsel shall stand, and I will do all** of **my pleasure:"*** (Isaiah 46:10; Enhanced)

* * *

*"**For we which have believed do enter into** the **rest** that has been provided by God. **As he said** before**, As I have sworn in my wrath, if they shall enter into my** finished **rest: although the works** of that rest **were finished from the foundation of the world."*** (Hebrews 4:3; Enhanced)

The centermost issue of all of creation is the granting of *Free-Will* as a gift from a loving Creator. God, out of love, has chosen to create various categories of moral beings, and He has granted them the gift of *Free-Will* so that they shall autonomously be able to choose what it is that they personally desire to do. They shall then be held accountable for their personal decisions, and rebellion against the common good and disobedience to non-grievous requirements shall be evaluated, and righteous judgment must be rendered where it is appropriate.

We are not as far into the collective net of created *Time* as is put forth by two-dimensional thinking, reprobate men, who desire to factor our loving God right out of the picture with their prognostications. Therefore, already established creative endeavors, various constituencies of *Free-Will* moral beings, and project development particulars should not be cataloged within the *billions and billions* or even the *millions and millions*-of-years envelope, as is put forth by these Hell-driven intellects who measure their indisputable *factual* findings by the very machines that they have created. In establishing what it is that an individual truly believes, Christians need to go to the immutable counsel of the Word of God and study out what the actual Creator of all things plainly declares.

There are numerous decisions and actions that have been taken by the Members of the Godhead to establish clarity and declare insight into Their own Personages, as well as provide a schematic of creative maneuvers that have occurred right up until NOW. Within that universal blueprint is the *Predestination* work of the cross.

The Members of the Godhead amicably decided amongst Themselves which One of the Persons would experience incarnation and become a MAN. They drafted a plan that was incorporated within the gifting of *Free-Will* provision. They collectively worked together on the project as God . . . Man . . . and Helper to accomplish the needed definitive dealing with the heinous Law of Sin and its consequences. Upon the resurrection of the Lord Jesus Christ of Nazareth, and the application of his Life-carrying blood upon the Mercy Seat in Heaven . . . the Plan was ratified. By its very design, any individual Human-Being that desires to partake of all of the benefits of that Plan need only choose to believe and accept what has been done. Upon a confirmation of that *belief,* the totality of what is incorporate within that entire Plan becomes theirs.

Therefore, what was once only a reality within the Realm of Thought, has transitioned into the Holy Scriptures and become a reality within the Realm of Word, and over a designated *period-of-time* has transitioned by actions and become a reality within the Realm of Deed . . . *Predestination.*

We are the inheritors of that magnificent Plan that was laid out so many millennia ago. The Omniscient God of all creation knew about you and I even before we were a gleam in our father's eye. We are among the privileged to be brought forth during this extremely narrow slice of *Time* in which this offer is made. Go forth, knowledgeable of who you are, and declare this gem of reality with all whom you meet.

    Jesus Christ of Nazareth is the visible agent of *Predestination.* **And all of the benefits within the Plan of Redemption are complete RIGHT NOW. They have been** *ESTABLISHED BY FAITH* **and shall become personally ours when we choose to** *ACTIVATE BY BELIEF* **that which has been done!**

SUPERNATURAL

CHAPTER 7

"Then came the disciples to Jesus apart, and said unto him, **Why could not we** *deal with this demon and cast him out?*

And Jesus said unto them, Because of your unbelief. For verily I say unto you the truth, If ye have the substance of **faith***, even as small as* **a grain of mustard seed, ye shall say unto this mountain, Remove hence** *unto a* **yonder place . . . and it shall remove! And nothing shall be impossible unto you."** *(Matthew 17:19-20; Enhanced)*

Here is a statement from a Man of spiritual knowledge and insight that carries with it no limitations. It is the volume of needed faith to accomplish a task that is the issue here, not the lack of it by the user. A *mustard-seed* grain of faith has enough power in it to relocate a mountain. *(The substance of Faith is one of the most powerful elements within God's creation. The Universe itself, and all things operative within it, were created utilizing words spoken in faith) (John 1:1-3; Mark 11:23-24; Romans 4:17)*

Jesus was fully aware of the reality that during the days in which he walked upon this planet, men were still held captive by Sin, and were still missing a full

1/3rd of their dimensional construct. But Jesus is not really ministering and teaching directly about that present day... but of the future to come... after his resurrection, and in particular, after his Second Coming.

Sadly, as Christians, we take spiritual realities far too lightly. We are still having too much *fun* living our lives from day to day, enjoying the blessings of being a Human-Being. We are so fully persuaded by the *natural (i.e. what we see, hear, taste, touch, and smell)*, that many times we ignore the *spiritual* until we literally trip over it. We are not going to be able to build our stockpile of *Faith* with what we hear on Sunday mornings in church, no matter how well the minister entertains us... or by what we talk about within weekly Bible study routines... or by what we obtain from our casual bed-side reading of the Word of God. We must become tenacious in our pursuit of *Faith*.

Should we find ourselves *in Christ*, because we have surrendered and put our trust in Jesus, then we are already legally considered Supernatural. The needed work has already been done... and by the way, it has not been done by us! We simply get to enjoy all of the benefits of someone else's labors.

The resurrection of Jesus of Nazareth from the spiritual and physical dead is a RIGHT NOW reality. The Universal Law of Life in Christ Jesus *(Romans 6:16)* altering the paralyzing effects of the Law of Sin is a

RIGHT NOW reality. The restoring of our missing 1/3rd spirit-dimension of our construct *(i.e. the Recreation of our spirit back unto Eternal Life)* is a RIGHT NOW reality. The putting-off-potential of our *Old Man* and the putting-on-potential of our *New Man* is a RIGHT NOW reality, but we are the ones who must *flesh-out* that process and manifest that reality in a personal manner.

We are the ones who hesitate and doubt! *(Mark 11:23)* We are the ones who are so fearful! *(Matthew 8:26)* We are the ones who do not really believe! *(Matthew 17:20)* We are the ones who do not **"calleth things which be not!"** *(Romans 4:17)* We are the ones who are not yet fully persuaded! *(Romans 4:21)* WHEN WILL IT BEGIN TO CHANGE?? Are we expecting God to override our free-will and MAKE US do something? Are we really believing that we will simply wake up one morning, and it will all be different, without us having to do anything? Where do we get such nonsense?

The Supernatural is a RIGHT NOW reality. We need to make the jump to light-speed and become the children of light that our Heavenly Father desires that we should be. No one is going to push us. No one is going to lead us by the hand. No one is going to do it for us. There is no such thing as POOF! Read and study the Word of God. Read and study the Word of God. Read and study the Word of God. That is how it is done. Increase in the knowledge of our God. *(Hosea 4:6; Colossians 1:10)* Read it again, and again, and again, and again. Memorize the Word. Meditate upon the Word. Purpose to make the Word of God the bottom-line of every decision and action within your life.

"So then the substance of **faith cometh by hearing** *from God,* **and hearing** *from God cometh* **by the Word of God."** *(Romans 10:17; Enhanced)*

<u>**ESTABLISHED BY FAITH**</u> from *Before the Beginning* . . . Personally <u>**ACTIVATED BY BELIEF**</u> . . . **<u>RIGHT NOW!</u>**

REDEEMED

CHAPTER 8

"And his father Zechariah was filled with the Holy Ghost, and prophesied, saying,

Blessed be the Lord God of Israel; for He hath visited and redeemed his people Israel even as He promised,

And hath raised up a horn of salvation, for the whole world, and for us, right in the midst of the House of his servant David;

As he spake by the mouth of his holy prophets, which have been ministering since the world began:"
(Luke 1:67-70; Enhanced)

* * *

"Christ hath redeemed us from the curse of the Law of Moses, being himself made a curse for us: for it is written, Cursed is every one that hangeth on a tree:

That the blessing of Abraham might come upon the Gentiles through Jesus Christ. That we might also receive the promise of the Spirit through faith." (Galatians 3:13-14; Enhanced)

* * *

"Forasmuch as ye know that ye were not redeemed with corruptible things,** such **as silver and gold, from your vain** religious **conversation received by** the **tradition from your fathers;

But with the precious blood of Christ, as of a lamb without blemish and without spot:

Who verily was foreordained** even **before the foundation of the world, but was** finally **manifest in these last times for you,

Who by him do believe in God, that raised him up from the** spiritual and physical **dead, and gave him glory; that your faith and hope might be** anchored **in God." *(I Peter 1:18-21; Enhanced)*

When we think of something that might need to be Redeemed . . . the local Pawn Shop many times comes to mind. At some point in time, for whatsoever reason, someone took an item into the Pawn Shop in exchange for monetary compensation. The Pawn Shop itself now owns that particular item . . . in its entirety.

In order to get that item back, it must be Redeemed. Someone who is not indebted to the Pawn Shop in any way must have the financial wherewithal be able to pay the price that is demanded by the new owner of the item, and must have the desire to Redeem that which is considered precious.

"For we know that the Law** of Moses **is** actually **spiritual, but** within spiritual-death **I am** still **carnal** and natural**, sold under sin." *(Romans 7:14; Enhanced)*

The Scriptures reveal that the first Human-Being named Adam exchanged his spiritual freedom and authority for the lusts of the flesh, *(Genesis 2:17; Romans 5:12, 7:14)* and in so doing became a servant, and sold the entire Human Race down the drain. *(Romans 6:16)*

When Jewish Jesus of Nazareth came to this Earth, he did so to Redeem the Nation of Israel that was in a Covenantial relationship with God, from the bondage of Sin. *(John 1:11; Galatians 4:4-5)* He did not come to Redeem the entire world at the first because God was not under Covenantial responsibility to anyone except the Nation of Israel. The rest of the world, at that time, was doomed to destruction and separation from God. *(John 3:19-20; Ephesians 2:12)*

However, on the cross, when Jesus declared that all things that needed to be accomplished by his First-Coming were completed . . . the picture then changed dramatically, and the whole world was extended the invitation to be redeemed from Sin's death grip. *(John 1:12 3:16, 19:28, 30)*

"And they sung a new song, saying, Thou art worthy to take the Book, and to open the seals *of* *the Book* **thereof. For thou was slain** *for all of Mankind,* **and hast Redeemed us** *unto* **God by thy** *precious* **blood out of every kindred, and tongue, and people, and nation.**

And hast made *of us,* **unto our God, kings and priests. And we shall reign on the earth** *with Christ Jesus."* *(Revelation 5:9-10; Enhanced)*

Today, we are the Redeemed! We are freed from the restraints of Sin and are able to effectively pray with confidence and obtain results. *(I John 3:21-22)* We are gloriously Redeemed by the Blood of the Lamb, **"slain from the foundation of the world."** *(Revelation 13:8)* We are under indebtedness to no one. We do not serve Sin any longer. The extended grace of God puts us in a commanding position, allowing us the opportunity to authoritatively **"calleth those things which be not as though they were."** *(Romans 4:17)*

Once again this is an already, RIGHT NOW, <u>ESTABLISHED BY FAITH</u> resurrection reality. We are not dealing with things that are *going* **to happen, but rather with things which have** *already* **happened two-thousand years ago. But even until this day, it is all still <u>*ACTIVATED BY BELIEF.*</u>**

RIGHTEOUSNESS OF GOD

CHAPTER 9

"But of him are all of ye who are in Christ Jesus, who of God the Father is made unto us wisdom, and righteousness, and sanctification, and redemption." (I Corinthians 1:30; Enhanced)

* * *

"And that ye put on the New Creation Man, which being patterned after God Himself is Recreated in righteousness and true holiness." (Ephesians 4:24; Enhanced)

* * *

"For he hath made him to actually be made Sin for us, who himself knew no sin; that we in turn might be made the righteousness of God in him." (II Corinthians 5:21; Enhanced)

In simplicity, the condition of *Righteousness* is the capacity to have the very *right* to stand before a holy, and innocent, and just, and *righteous* God without reservation. However, from the disobedient moment of Sin's acidic effect upon the express image creation of God, known as Adam, God's finest endeavor became unholy, and unjust, and guilty and unrighteous before his Maker. And all of this ugliness was passed on down the road unto us through Human reproduction. *(Romans 3:23; 5:12)* And within this Divinely designed universe, unholiness is not allowed to live in holiness . . . and that which is guilty is not allowed to live with that which is innocent . . . and the unjust are not allowed to live with those that are just . . . and the unrighteous are not allowed to live with those who are righteous. Since God created this expanse to house creatures that are holy, and innocent, and just, and right before Him . . . because of what the Law of Sin has influenced and affected, He has quite a clean-up project ahead of Him.

The very issue of *Righteousness* is actually a two-edged sword with both a spiritual-edge and a practical-edge. The spiritual-edge of the blade has to do with the reality condition of the individual. So . . . is the individual alive or dead? Is the individual pregnant or not pregnant? Is the individual righteous or unrighteous? There is no middle ground.

When we actually came forth into existence the world that we were birthed into was already saturated with unrighteousness. Sin abounded everywhere that you looked and the very concept of right-standing, or *Righteousness*, was foreign unto us. We were birthed into a puddle of mud, and since we grew up within the mud, the mud seemed to be quite the norm for us.

When we first even hear of the issue of *Righteousness* it is a foreign concept unto our ears. Nothing around us seems to be at all *right* so how can we expect to be *right* ourselves when nothing else is? And then we hear about Jesus. We hear about a man who for all intents and purposes is a complete stranger to us. A man, whom we are told, that was willing to give up his very life for people he did not even know. Should we choose to surrender unto the preaching of the gospel, our deceased, missing $1/3^{rd}$ dimension of our spirit is restored unto us and, the concept of *Righteousness* now takes on new light and becomes understandable. The actual work that desperately needed to take place is performed by Jesus Christ of Nazareth, and our simple acceptance of what he has done grants unto us the blade-edge gifting of spiritual *Righteousness* before our *righteous* God... one half of the sword complete.

"And if the Righteous scarcely be saved *from destruction***, where shall the ungodly and the sinner appear** *at the judgment?***"** *(I Peter 4:18; Enhanced)*

* * *

"Little children, let no man deceive you *with the traditions of men which maketh the Word of God of none effect:* **he that** *actually* **doeth Righteousness is righteous, even as he is righteous."** *(I John 3:7; Enhanced)*

On the practical side, it comes down to our own personal actions. We cannot continue with unrighteous thinking and expect God to wink and ignore it, and not hold us accountable. We cannot continue with foul, heinous, lying and unrighteous words issuing forth from our lips and expect God to turn a deaf ear and ignore it, and not hold us accountable. And we cannot continue with our reprobate and disobedient actions and expect that God will lovingly pay no attention to it, and not hold us accountable.

"He that doeth Righteousness is righteous" establishes the epicenter of the second blade-edge of the Sword of *Righteousness*. Our behavior does matter, and we must best understand that before it is too late. For those who teach the false doctrine of Eternal-Security, i.e. that once you are saved by the grace of God *(Ephesians 2:8)* and the faith of Jesus *(John 1:12)* it does not really matter what you do, because your issuance into Heaven is assured ... you had better read the Book again. Nowhere within the Scriptural account does it declare that your *future sins* are forgiven. Your past sins are forgiven, *(Romans 3:25)* yes ... and you are able to confess your current sins if there are any, *(I John 1:9)* yes ... but you should not be planning for *future sins* because you are now supposed to be a child of light, and walk in that light, *(I John 1:7)* and not continue to be a child of darkness.

So, concerning the two-edged Sword of *Righteousness*, the first edge is accomplished by Christ and is gifted unto us ... and the second edge is accomplished by us and puts us into a right standing position before our God.

All of this is once again, <u>ESTABLISHED BY FAITH</u> and personally acquired for each and every one of us by our own *<u>ACTIVATION BY BELIEF.</u>*

MORE THAN A CONQUEROR

CHAPTER 10

"Nay, in all of these troubling things concerning the issues-of-life, we are more than conquerors through him that loved us." (Romans 8:37; Enhanced)

Complete, Triumphant, Glorious, Overwhelming Victory is what this verse proclaims. Words of encouragement from a God of grace who has done mighty things on behalf of those whom He loves.

It is reported by historians that in strategic battles between soldiers of previous empires . . . that *to the victor went the spoils.* The winning commander was received into his capital city regaled in his finest raiment. He rode in the lead chariot and was preceded by beautiful maidens tossing fragrant flower blossoms before him. The trumpeters and the other musicians sounded a loud marching tune, and there were admiring citizens boisterously cheering the victor along his corridor of honor.

Meanwhile, the loser of the campaign is being dragged behind the victor tightly bound within painful chains of iron. His tattered uniform belies his defeat, and a multitude of jeers are heaped upon him by the antagonistic crowd. If he had been fortunate, he would have been slain in the battle. As it is, he must endure the disdain, and shoulder the shame of defeat before every single person within the city.

In the very real conflict that occurred between the Human-Being incarnate of Deity, whom we know of as Jesus Christ of Nazareth, and the upstart, angelic, fallen prince of the kingdom of darkness, whom we know of as Satan . . . the victory was resounding.

"And having spoiled *the wicked, fallen,* **principalities and powers, he made a show of them openly** *before the entire Realm of the Spirit,* **triumphing** *victoriously* **over them in it."** *(Colossians 2:15; Enhanced)*

* * *

"I am he that liveth *again,* **and was** *both spiritually and physically* **dead, and, behold, I am** *now* **alive forevermore, Amen. And** *now* **I have the keys of Hell and of Death."** *(Revelation 1:18; Enhanced)*

But please note . . . that when the preliminaries of serious conflict began, the picture did not look very good for Jesus, at all.

He was rejected by Human stooges of the Devil throughout his entire life on this Earth. He stepped into public ministry but was resisted by doubt and unbelief at every turn. Hatred and jealousy of his success with the unheralded men and women of the masses escalated to a crescendo and concluded when he was finally arrested during a time of respite and prayer. Dragged before a series of religious elders he was mocked, ridiculed, challenged, insulted, and shamed. Finally, he was tortured and scourged, bore a woven crown of 2" Judean thorns, had his hands and feet pierced with 2 lb. iron spikes, and hung suspended on a cross, gasping for breath with every inhale.

In addition to his grievous physical maladies, he was spiritually swallowed up by Sin's acidic depth of wretchedness and finally succumbed to Death's delight. All aspects of spiritual Life were sucked from his Personage. All evidence of spiritual Light was brutally snuffed out by reason of the overwhelming prevailing darkness. Only his unfailing spiritual Love remained unmoved and untouched.

The original HuMAN-Being testator was declared obliterated, *(Hebrews 9:26)* and echoes of delight reverberated from every corner of the Region of the Nether World. For all intents and purposes, it would appear to any observing bystander that the one hope for this world, which was sent to us from Heaven, was unsuccessful in his attempt to wrest authoritative control out of the hands of the Devil.

* * *

For seventy-one hours, fifty-nine minutes, and fifty-nine seconds of prophetically fulfilled, operational-*Time*, commencing from the settling-in of the rolled-stone into place, silence brooded over the discernibly dank sepulcher upon this Earth.

Within the darkness of the Realm of the Nether World, no sound could be heard uttering forth from silenced lips of Love. All of the heinousness that Hell could muster had been heaped upon *Flesh-Suited* Deity by the contentious head-rebel of ultimate hatred, in an attempt to annihilate any possible residue of mercy and compassion. There are no known words capable of describing the bottomless depth of darkness and hopelessness concerning that of which we are talking. The seemingly apparent summation would be that the totality, of harmony and creative love which prevailed over this Universe, is now lost . . . forever.

* * *

The arrival of the Holy Spirit of God within the bowels of the Region of Utter-Darkness must have been quite a shock to the milling residents therein. Queried wonderment instantaneously turns into abject horror as the Super-Nova detonation of **New-Life**-impartation fills the first **Born-Again** spirit of the MAN Jesus Christ of Nazareth. *(Colossians 1:15, 18; Revelation 3:14)* **"The power of his resurrection"** *(Philippians 3:10)* immediately blows all of the citizens of Hell flat on their back. Unquestioned authority promptly strips Satan of all instruments of power and prestige, and brain-washed minds still reel from the confusion and grapple at trying to understand what has just happened.

Divinely impressed directives clearly explain to the entire population of the Nether World, the reality of the total crushing defeat that their totalitarian leader has just experienced. All of Hell now knows of his utterly failed bodaciousness.

* * *

We now, in total fullness, are the blessed beneficiaries of this accomplished victory. His triumph, by personal identification, has become our triumph! He did all of the necessary hard work, and we reap the delightful fruits of his labors. We no longer need to put up with the shenanigans of the supreme murdering liar; we are capable of calling his bluff and dismissing him. **_ESTABLISHED BY FAITH_** and personally **_ACTIVATED BY BELIEF!_**

When we read that we are *more* than a conqueror it means that we not only obtain the victory but we further rub the nose of the loser in the quagmire of his defeat. We do not simply walk away as the winner, but we make sure that the loser knows what a loser he is. We rub his nose in it again, and again, and again!

SIN FREE

CHAPTER 11

"Being then made completely free from sin, ye became the servants of righteousness." (Romans 6:18; Enhanced)

* * *

"But now being made completely free from sin, and become servants unto God, ye have your spiritual fruit unto holiness, and the end of your journey is Everlasting Life." (Romans 6:22; Enhanced)

* * *

"For the law of the Holy Spirit, of Life in Christ Jesus, hath made me free from the Law of Sin and the consequences of Death that come with it." (Romans 8:2; Enhanced)

* * *

"In whom we have complete redemption through his shed blood, the forgiveness of all of our sins, according to the riches of his unmerited grace." (Ephesians 1:7; Enhanced)

The Law of Sin is the most heinous reality within creation, and the cruelest taskmaster operating inside of the entire expanse of space. Sin is not a person or a concept, but rather the totality of negativity functioning within a creatively positive Universe. In simplistic and understandable terms, its' very existence is a result of deserved gifted anointing *(Ezekiel 28:14-15)* knowingly combined with *Free-Will* disobedience. *(Isaiah 14:13-14)* And when that unholy union occurred, the Law of Sin instantly burst forth into manifestation, and the very first victim and still number one captive to that Law was the very author of all rebellion and disobedience... the once *Holy*, but now *Fallen-Angel* Satan. The Law of Sin is similar to a giant electrical short-circuit, causing havoc within a huge well-oiled machine of benevolence and good-will. Sin is acidically compulsive and contagious. We are given an insight into the actual workings of the Law of Sin by the *Revelation* that the Apostle Paul received from the risen Lord Jesus Christ.

> **"For that** *thing* **which I** *desire to* **do, I** *choose to* **allow not. For what I would** *really want to do*, **that do I not. But what I** *actually* **hate** *to do*, **that do I.**
> **If then I do that which I would** *really* **not** *want to do*, **I consent unto the Law** *of Moses* **that it is good** *in revealing Sin unto me.*

Now then it is *actually* **no more I that** *personally* **do it, but** *the reality of* **Sin that** *I allow to continue to* **dwelleth in me.**

For I know that *with***in me** *personally* **(that is,** *with***in my** *unredeemed* **flesh,) dwelleth no good thing. For** *the desire* **to will is present with me; but how to** *actually* **perform that which is good I find not.**

For the good that I would *want to do***, I do not. But the evil which I would not** *want to do***, that I do.**

Now if I do that *which* **I would not** *want to do***, it is** *truthfully* **no more I that do it, but Sin that** *I allow to continue to* **dwelleth** *with***in me.**

I find then a Law, that, when I would *want to* **do good, evil is** *still* **present with me.**

For I delight in the Law of God, *which is the Royal Law*, **after the inward** *spiritual* **man.**

But I see another Law *operating with***in my members** *which is the Law of the Flesh*, **warring against the Royal Law of** *God within* **my mind, and bringing me into captivity** *and bondage* **to the Law of Sin which is** *allowed to continue to operate with***in my members.**

O wretched man that I am! Who shall deliver me from the *unredeemed* **body of this Death?**

I thank God *that* **through Jesus Christ our Lord** *I am now liberated from the Law of Sin*. **So then with the mind I myself** *choose to* **serve the Law of God** *which is* *the Royal Law; **but within the** unredeemed **flesh the Law of Sin** still rages."* *(Romans 7:15-25; Enhanced)*

Active operating Sin <u>*should*</u> *not* be allowed to continue to go unchecked. We are not under the Law of Moses anymore, but rather under Grace. *(Romans 6:14)* We <u>*should*</u> *not* continue to obey the dictates of the flesh and of the mind. *(Romans 6:16)* We are now able to do all things through Christ which strengtheneth us *(Philippians 4:13)* and when we are tempted, we need to submit ourselves therefore unto God, *(James 4:7)* and resist the Devil and the Law of Sin that he continually attempts to use against us.

* * *

The Divine correction that needed to take place as far as definitively dealing with the Law of Sin was a two-part process. The first part needed to be the dealing with of the author of that heinous Law . . . and the second part would be the dealing with of the very Law itself.

The two initial moral creations that God brought forth are the Creation Category of *Angels (originally only Holy)*, and the Creation Category of *Other Creatures*. *(Romans 8:39)*

Holy Angels are an all male gender society, without reproductive permission, who are in a designated position of willful servitude within a multitude of vocational arenas, assisting and ministering primarily unto God, and then unto Man when he is brought forth.

Unholy Angels are an all male gender, restricted, renegade band of *principalities, powers, rulers of the darkness of this world, and wicked spirits adversely affecting the Heavenly places* of this planet Earth. *(Ephesians 6:12)* The most notorious Fallen-Angelic individual is a spirit-being originally named Lucifer, but known of today because of his Sin-changed nature, as Satan.

Other Creatures are an unknown gender society, with unknown reproductive permission, and they occupy a third position moral creation status. They inhabit various planets throughout this universe, *(Colossians 1:16)* and in the case of the planet Earth, were the first inhabitants that ultimately supported and joined the once Holy Angel that was installed in a governance position over them.

* * *

The Law of Sin was originally birthed upon this planet Earth because of the willful disobedience and rebellion of the prideful Angelic governor set into a position of development perfection. *(Ezekiel 28:15)*

The original Angelic Probationary Period, which is the first probation of all moral creation, ended with the Judgment and restriction of the Angelic governor of the planet Earth, and his assistant Angelic constituents from various other locales within the expanse of space ... and the first inhabitant *Other Creatures* that he ruled over, and persuaded to accompany him in his quest for supreme rulership of this Universe. *(Isaiah 14:13)* The end result was that the planet Earth was flooded with water for the first time *(Psalms 104:6)*, the ambient light from the already existing Sun, the Moon, and the Stars was withheld *(Jeremiah 4:23)*, decreed destruction of the societal presence was total *(Jeremiah 4:24-26)*, and the God of creative love left the room, only to return at an undesignated future point in time to begin another work. The conclusion of this Judgmental process brought to an end the first phase dealing with the author of the Law of Sin.

* * *

The second phase of the process of definitively dealing with the Law of Sin itself is a work handled entirely by the incarnated God-Man named Jesus Christ of Nazareth.

Right at the outset of a New creative work begun by God, taking place on the planet Earth, the active operating aspect of the Law of Sin is once again allowed to function freely for the second time. *(Romans 5:12)* The whole of Mankind is subjected to enslavement, and the supreme condition that Man was created in, begins to decline on a steady basis. Granted authority

(Genesis 1:28; Psalms 8:3-5; Hebrews 2:8) was never altered, and Satan usurped men and held the reigns until the sacrifice of Jesus of Nazareth.

As the <u>only</u> Human-Being not under the control of Sin, Jesus allows himself to actually become Sin in an exchange program that was executed right out in the open for everyone within both the visible realm and the invisible realm to witness. When that work concludes Jesus is raised up from the Spiritual and Physical Dead, and the chains of bondage that held men captive for so long are smashed to pieces.

The behavior modifying Law of Moses still remains in place but unrestricted grace blankets the planet Earth, and every individual no matter their race, color, or creed is offered an opportunity to leave all the of old rubbish of their life behind and become an integral part of something brand New.

The Law of Sin is still in existence, but a gracious Creator grants a two-thousand-year window of *time* for men to decide for Everlasting spiritual liberty from the bonds of Sin or to hold fast to their stubbornness and technically remain spiritually Mortal for an Eternity to come. The program of definitively dealing with the unprecedented Law of Sin is fully complete, and we are in the final stages of drafting Universe Ruling constituents from the ranks of the Human-Being populous on planet Earth.

The totality of the magnitude of this Sin-Freeing endeavor has singularly been accomplished and *__ESTABLISHED BY FAITH__* through the work of the Lord Jesus Christ of Nazareth. The only missing ingredient is for it to be individually *__ACTIVATED BY BELIEF.__*

ABLE TO DO ALL THINGS

CHAPTER 12

"I can now do all things through Christ which strengtheneth me." (Philippians 4:13; Enhanced)

What an open-ended statement! Our hearts should leap at the thought of what this verse of Scripture reveals unto us. No limitations. No boundaries. No short-comings. This verse is right up there with the uncharted territory of **"nothing shall be impossible unto you."** (Matthew 17:20)

Currently, we live within a naturally-visible world of limitations. Everything around us demonstrates a boarder of *cease your forward movement.* We have become so familiar and fully persuaded with boundaries and limitations that our mind virtually balks at the thought of the unrestricted.

When we first hear of the possibility of it, within our newly recreated *Born-Again* Human spirit, we excitedly race right up to the edge of the challenge, and then our soulish, carnal, natural brain kicks-in, and we slam on the brakes and screechingly think . . . Wait . . . ! I can't do that!

We need to seriously purpose and press-in to get ourselves past the natural. Legally speaking, we are not natural anymore. *In Christ,* we are Supernatural, by God's design and determination. Within our current natural thinking and reasoning, we shackle ourselves with *justifiable cause* as to why it cannot be done. Who says that it cannot be done if God says that it can? Within the RIGHT NOW, it is imperative that we shake-off the natural-limiting-concept of restriction if we want to take advantage of the privileges that God has afforded us by being *in Christ.*

A mind truly renewed on the Word of God will be able to take us to this very real world of what is now only *imagination.* And please understand, there is a tremendous difference between *imagination* and *fantasy. Imagination* is God-given, and it is directly connected to Creative-Vision. *Imagination* is the allowing of stated Truth to be viably envisioned at, what is now, an extreme perspective. God gave unto men free will and intellect in order for them to Create right alongside Him within the forever and ever after. Quality Father/Son, or Father/Daughter, time together, amidst Divine-family activities.

Fantasy, on the other hand, mimics *imagination,* but it is directly connected to falsehood. Two-dimensional men, who do not know where they have come from, or why they are here, are deeply steeped in *fantasy.* They live a "normal" natural life amidst their varied Earthly cultures . . . they hear, through one means or another of He who is known of as *God*... be it the One True God or one of a plethora of false gods... they know within their heart that there is something more out there than just this natural world that they live in... and they *fantasize* of where they will go when life on this Earth is over... launching themselves through a veil of ornately decorated *fantasy*... only to have the real Truth smack them right in the face at the time of their physical death... with the father-of-lies laughing as they are dragged down into a fiery torment that was originally prepared only for the Devil and his rebellious angels. *(Matthew 25:41)*

The Way-of-the-World is a yellow-brick road of *fantasy*. Those who are Worldly-Wise are also engaged in *fantasy*. Those in this life that are considered Street-Smart are students of *fantasy*. Politics, within the United States of America, is a quagmire of *fantasy*. The Entertainment Industry and its participants revel continually within *fantasy*. All Religion, except for Judaism *(which was established by the One True God)*, is a breeding-ground of *fantasy*. And since there is only one Truth, anything that is not the Truth must be a lie... so it follows that all lies find their roots-of-residency within *fantasy*.

And sadly, even genuine Christians, at least within the United States of America are racing down the road of *fantasy*. Even though the prophet Hosea has told us, **"my people are destroyed by lack of knowledge"**

(Hosea 4:6) it does not seem to matter. It must be the "other guy" that is going to be destroyed . . . not me! I'm *Born-Again*, and I love Jesus. I go to church and have several Scripture verses memorized. I'm active in church projects, and I just *know* that when I die, I am going to go to Heaven. *(Isn't it wonderful that God has sent all of those different Bible Translations directly from Heaven, so that I can pick the one that is the easiest to read, and that I am the most comfortable with? Isn't it wonderful that I do not have to tithe to my local church because that is an Old Testament doctrine and I simply get to determine what I want to do with my money? Isn't it wonderful that I can choose my Life-Partner and I do not have to enter into a Covenant because my love is stronger and more powerful than what the Bible says? Isn't it wonderful that I can simply believe whatsoever I choose to believe about God, and about what God has said, because, in the end, God will cause that the Universe will change its operations to line-up with what I choose to believe? Isn't it wonderful that I can still maintain my bad attitudes, and foul mouth, and unforgiveness, and carnality, and false doctrines, and damage my body as I see fit, and continue to enjoy the lusts of the flesh and of the mind? Isn't <u>fantasy</u> wonderful?)*

* * *

The extreme perspective has so much more reality attached to it; however, we will turn our attention to the practical aspect of being able to ***"do all things through Christ which strengtheneth me".*** *(Philippians 4:13)*

We have had more than our fill of excuses . . . but with this one verse, that luxury now comes to an end. Bad habits are no longer in a position to govern me . . . since I can now break those habits, ***"through Christ which strengtheneth me."*** Defeatist thinking is not able to overpower and control me anymore . . . since I can choose to renew my mind, ***"through Christ which strengtheneth me."*** Smoking, drinking, inappropriate sexual activity, tattooing, drugging, lying and foul language are no longer issues that I need to "struggle" with . . . because I can be completely victorious ***"through Christ which strengtheneth me."***

Should we not avail ourselves of this RIGHT NOW blessing, here on this Earth, then when do we plan to deal with these issues . . . When we go to Heaven? The strength does not come from us, it comes from Christ Jesus. He definitively dealt with the Law of Sin and broke-the-back of Sin's power. That is now available to us as believers *in Christ*. We must set our face like a flint. We must develop a vision for continual success. We must desire to move to a higher level than the world around us.

Fortunately, all of these victorious positions have been procured by the risen Lord of Glory, Jesus of Nazareth, <u>BY FAITH</u> . . . and we are able to access them RIGHT NOW with **_PERSONAL BELIEF ACTIVATION._** Let us delay no longer. Let us stop the procrastination! Do not simply read these words . . . act on them!

PREDESTINATED
CHAPTER 13

"For whom he did foreknow *from before the foundation of the world,* ***he also did predestinate to be*** *precisely* ***conformed to the*** *interior* ***image of his*** *Only Begotten* ***Son, that he might be the firstborn among*** *the* ***many brethren*** *that will come.*

Moreover, whom he did *choose to* ***predestinate*** *through Foreknowledge,* ***them he also called*** *to this exalted position.* ***And whom he called*** *to this exalted position,* ***them he also justified*** *and declared to be not guilty through the work of the cross.* ***And whom he justified*** *and declared to be not guilty through the work of the cross,* ***them he also glorified*** *to be the gods that they were created to be in the first place. (Psalms 82:6)"* *(Romans 8:29-30; Enhanced)*

To this author, there is not a more exciting set of verses within the whole of the context of the New Testament account than these.

When it comes to *Predestination*, the only valid Scriptural example has to do with the totality of the Plan of Redemption . . . which ranges from Before the Beginning unto the Resurrection from the Dead of the incarnated God-Man Jesus Christ of Nazareth.

The very epicenter of all of creation is the *Free Will* volition that God has granted unto the Moral-creature handiwork of His hands. If there is no *Free-Will* granted by God to His creation, then the purpose behind any Moral-creation becomes a moot point. If there is no Moral-creation even involved within His endeavors, then the purpose behind the very creation of this entire Universe becomes a moot point.

* * *

Predestination begins Before the Beginning when the only reality of existence was the Personage of God. Within the Scripturally declared Godhead, *(Acts 17:29; Romans 1:20; Colossians 2:9)* there are Three Persons. Utilizing the Foreknowledge portion of Omniscience, a Plan of Redemption was drafted for any of the wayward God-class creatures that would become known of as HuMan-Beings that the Lord God would ultimately bring forth **in** His own image and **after** His own likeness in the due process of *Time*. Man's position within creation was absolutely unprecedented and even today is not fully understood or accepted . . . even though God is the One who created Man in the first place, and states within the immutable counsel of His Word the reality of Truth.

Predestination is a Divinely designed program that is lovingly handcrafted in liquid silver and selectively dipped in transparent gold with a value that is beyond calculation. The Creator of all things has purposed to create another spirit-being as an *Express Image*, *(Hebrews 1:3)* exact duplication of Himself. Only the non-transferables of Omniscience, Omnipotence, Omnipresence, and Self-Existence from Everlasting will separate the One and Only Living God from His exquisite doppelganger handiwork. *(Even as these words are being read by you, there is a resistance to accept them as accurate.)* Through Foreknowledge, it is known that this unprecedented creature will deviate from the path of Righteousness and Holiness and almost immediately wander off into the forest of darkness.

Predestination is able to actually exist because all of the participants of the program are unchanging and without flaw. The Members of the Godhead and only the Members of the Godhead are involved in the program . . . with One of Them having to become a Man in order to execute the work to its fullness. Granted *Free Will* is indeed involved when the Second Person of the Godhead becomes a HuMan-Being, but the spiritual strength and resolve to see the entire project through without falling prey to the Law of Sin is able to be called upon, and for Jesus the Man to become fully persuaded concerning the victorious outcome. That same strength and resolve is now available for any Man or Woman, who has become Sin-Free and has been granted access to the unwavering inner strength that comes from the risen from the dead Man, Jesus Christ of Nazareth.

Predestination is God's personal plan to fabricate an invisible mold, to produce another god-being, *(Psalms 82:6; John 10:34)* who is conformed into the precise Xerox of His own Personage . . . within all three dimensions of his spirit, and his soul, and his likeness body. The person of a HuMan-Being that will singularly lack the four non-transferable qualities of Omniscience, and Omnipotence, and Omnipresence, and Self-Existence from Everlasting . . . and will actually constitute His very own family of sons and daughters.

* * *

We find ourselves a participant within a program that was not imagined, nor designed, by us . . . but affords us the opportunity to become Little-g sons and daughters of our Big-G Father. We did not have to do any of the work to successfully add to or fulfill that project. We simply need to surrender to the reality of declared Truth and renew our minds to comprehend the totality of that reality.

The risen Lord Jesus of Nazareth is the operative agent that has completely fulfilled the exquisite beauty of *Predestination*. He has <u>ESTABLISHED</u>

it ***BY FAITH,*** and has placed it before all of Hu-Man-ity for personal ***ACTIVATION BY BELIEF.***

IMMORTAL

CHAPTER 14

*"But it is now made manifest by the very appearing of our Saviour Jesus Christ, who hath abolished both Spiritual and Physical **Death** for those who will receive it, and hath brought Eternal **Life and Immortality to light through the gospel.**" (II Timothy 1:10; Enhanced)*

* * *

"Behold, I show you a Revelation mystery; we shall not all sleep in Physical Death, but we shall all be changed,

In a moment, in the twinkling of an eye, at the sound of the last trumpet: for the trumpet shall sound, and the Physically Dead shall be raised Incorruptible, and we which are alive and remain shall be changed. (I Thessalonians 4:16-17)

For this corruptible flesh must put on Incorruption, and this mortal condition must put on Immortality.

So when this corruptible flesh shall have put on Incorruption, and this mortal condition shall have put on Immortality, then shall be brought to pass the saying that is written by Isaiah the prophet, Death is swallowed up in victory. (Isaiah 25:8)

O death, where is thy sting? O grave, where is thy victory? *(I Corinthians 15:51-55; Enhanced)*

Immortality . . . is the dream of all young children, and also of most of the adult persons, among the Human-Being species of creation here on planet Earth. It is the opportunity that is afforded for one to physically live forever and ever and ever. To no longer be plagued anymore by the thought of personal Physical Death, and the separation from loved ones that Death brings, and the pain and heartache accompanying that condition.

Most people, at this particular point in time, whether Christian or non-Christian, would not know what to do with Immortality . . . which is probably why there is not too much excitement about it when the subject comes up for discussion. By-the-way, what are you going to do with it?

In addition, so that there will be a clear understanding . . . *<u>Immortality</u> is a State of Existence . . . of not being able to be touched or affected by the condition of either Spiritual or Physical Death in any of its manifestations.* The risen Lord of Glory, Jesus of Nazareth, has provided for that rare opportunity of existing within that State of Immortality, for any Human-Being that will receive it . . . but it is a *limited-time*-offer extended unto men only within a very short 2000 year window-of-opportunity of Probationary *Time* within the whole spectrum of Eternity.

* * *

The Scripture verses that are quoted above are a Divine Revelation of encouragement... presented to prospective children of the Most High God. Once again... within today's society, all around us, from moment to moment there is the overwhelming shouting of *Natural! Natural! Natural...! Death! Death! Death...! It's Over! It's Over! It's Over...! No More! No More! No More...! Termination! Termination! Termination!* However, Jesus Christ has dealt with all of those limitations and has opened a wide door to an expanse of growth and to eons of unending Life.

* * *

Just think of it . . . you can fly right through a Black Hole in outer space because you are Immortal and cannot die. You are not mandated to have to eat any kind of food for survival anymore because you are Immortal and cannot die. You can fly throughout outer-space to anyplace within this Universe that you would like to go, without needing a spacesuit or oxygen, because you are Immortal and cannot die. You are able to confront and defeat any opposing force or creature without hesitation or fear because you are

Immortal and cannot die. You can do anything that your mind or your heart can imagine because you are Immortal and cannot die. And this offer of Immortality is so magnanimous that the current *natural-thinking* mind is unable to wrap itself around it.

This reality of Immortality is *off the charts*. This reality of Immortality is *beyond belief*. This reality of Immortality is *too good to be true*. This reality of Immortality is considered *unimaginable*. We love the idea, but we choose to believe that it is a *fantasy*, and will not truly grasp hold of it. We revel in the potential of it, but we will not allow ourselves to accept it as being so. And the question ultimately becomes... Which is it? Whose report will we believe? Sadly, that is where our greatest difficulty comes in... with all of the *Pauline Revelation* statements that are made in the New Testament. We need to make the *jump to light speed*. We need to abandon our old *limitation* ideas and accept the declaration of Truth. We need to really recognize that we are not the same old person that we once were before we became *Born-Again*. That is where this all started. Without the *New Birth* we are just like every other Human-Being that is on this planet named Earth, **"being aliens from the** *Covenant* **commonwealth of Israel, and strangers from** *all of the* *extended* **Covenants of promise,** *in reality* **having no hope** *for the future,* **and without God in the world".** *(Ephesians 2:12; Enhanced)*

But as a New Creature in Christ, we are not the same anymore. We are now different. And it is that difference that we have been talking about throughout this entire little work. Let's make the effort to change.

Remember that all of these promises are an already _ESTABLISHED WORK OF FAITH_ that can only become a reality by personal _ACTIVATION THROUGH BELIEF._

CHRIST-MINDED

CHAPTER 15

"For who hath known the mind of the Lord? Or who hath been his counselor?" (Romans 11:34)

* * *

"For who hath known the mind of the Lord, that he may instruct him? But we have the mind of Christ." (I Corinthians 2:16)

* * *

"And be renewed in the spirit of your mind." (Ephesians 4:23)

* * *

"Let this mind be in you, which was also in Christ Jesus.

Who, being in the form of God, thought it not robbery to be equal with God:" (Philippians 2:5-6)

* * *

"Forasmuch then as Christ hath suffered for us in the flesh, arm yourselves with the same mind: for he that hath suffered in the flesh hath ceased from sin;" (I Peter 4:1)

What was running through the mind of the Human-Being, Jewish Jesus of Nazareth, from his early toddler formation days, right up until the time of the Passover Celebration Event that we witness when he was twelve years of age? *(Luke 2:46-50)*

What was running through the mind of the Human-Being, Jewish Jesus of Nazareth, from the time of the Holy Spirit *Revelation*, at that Passover Celebration Event, that he was actually God manifest in the flesh . . . through the next eighteen years of his life? *(Philippians 2:8)*

What was running through the mind of the Human-Being, Jewish Jesus of Nazareth, at the time of his Temptation in the Wilderness, by Satan the archenemy of God? *(Luke 4:1-13)*

What was running through the mind of the Human-Being, Jewish Jesus of Nazareth, as he was ministering with power among men, through the direction and empowering of the Holy Spirit of God and His giftings? *(Matthew, Mark, Luke, John)*

What was running through the mind of the Human-Being, Jewish Jesus of Nazareth, as he anguished over the lost souls of men, and the exorbitant price that was going to have to be paid to liberate them from their disobedience and rebellion, as he prayed in the Garden of Gethsemane on the night of his arrest? *(Matthew 26:36-46; Mark 14:32-42; Luke 22:39-46)*

What was running through the mind of the Human-Being, Jewish Jesus of Nazareth, as his life-long companion, the Holy Spirit of God, departed from him and the talons of Sin, Death, and Hell came piercing down upon him, as he hung suspended on a rugged cross just outside of the walls of the City of Jerusalem on an early Wednesday morning? *(Matthew 27:45-50; Mark 15:33-37; Luke 23:33-46; John 19:26-30)*

<u>What was running through *his* mind?</u>

* * *

For us to truly understand the reality of being *Christ-Minded*, we must first of all understand about **The Christ**.

The Christ, which Scripturally refers to the particular individual that shall become The Anointed One of God, must qualify for that position by actually belonging to the created species of Human-Being.

Next, the particular individual must further qualify by being in a legally binding Blood-Covenant relationship with the Creator of the Universe.

Additionally, the particular individual that qualifies for the position of **The Christ <u>cannot</u>** be imprisoned in any way, by the shackles and compulsions that exist concerning *The Law of Sin,* or the *Spiritual-Death* that emanates forth from disobedience and rebellion.

During the days of an incarnated Human-Being, named Jesus of Nazareth, there is only One particular individual that is able to meet the qualifications for the position of becoming **The Christ**.

Jesus of Nazareth, **The Christ**, was not hindered by the fear of failure, intimidation, unworthiness, inability, or of thoughts of not being qualified. He was the MAN that God sent to be *The Answer* to all of the questions, concerns, and uncertainties that saturated the planet Earth. He did not anguish over the idea of not knowing everything because he intimately walked with the Person of the Holy Spirit of God, who indeed does know everything. There was no challenge that remained unmet with him.

So . . . <u>What was running through *his* mind?</u>

* * *

To be *Christ-Minded* literally means . . . to remove all of the mental restrictions that present themselves as valid . . . but are really not!

Jesus of Nazareth did not consider himself to be a sinner because he was not a sinner. Jesus of Nazareth did not have to deal with **"*old things are passed away*"** because there were not any old things for him to be distracted with. Jesus of Nazareth (functioning as a MAN) did not consider it robbery to be equal with God because he *was* equal by God's own design.

Jesus of Nazareth did not allow the *Realm of the Natural* to dictate their circumstances to him, in order to try and stop him from what he was directed to do by his loving Heavenly Father. Jesus of Nazareth did not operate <u>under</u> the deluge of circumstances that presented themselves, but rather purposed to rise <u>above</u> all that is seen, heard, tasted, touched, or smelled, in order to see clearly and do what was needed to be done.

Jesus of Nazareth fulfilled all of the conditions of qualification to walk and operate as **The Christ** while he was here on this Earth.

∗ ∗ ∗

"Among whom are ye also <u>the called</u> of Jesus Christ:" *(Romans 1:6; Enhanced)*

∗ ∗ ∗

"Even <u>the righteousness of God</u> which is by faith of Jesus Christ <u>unto all</u> and upon all them <u>that believe</u>; for there is no difference; *(Romans 3:22; Enhanced)*

∗ ∗ ∗

Being <u>justified freely</u> by his grace <u>through</u> the redemption that is in <u>Christ Jesus</u>:" *(Romans 3:24; Enhanced)*

∗ ∗ ∗

"For if by one man's offense death reigned by one; <u>much more they which receive abundance of</u>

<u>grace and of the gift of righteousness shall reign in life</u> by one, Jesus Christ." *(Romans 5:17; Enhanced)*

* * *

"Know ye not, that so many of us as were <u>baptized into Jesus Christ</u> were baptized into his death?

Therefore we are buried with him by baptism into death: that like as Christ was raised up from the dead by the glory of the Father, even so we also should walk in newness of Life." *(Romans 6:3-4; Enhanced)*

* * *

"<u>But of him are ye in Christ Jesus</u>, who of God is made unto us wisdom, and righteousness, and sanctification, and redemption." *(I Corinthians 1:30; Enhanced)*

* * *

"For who hath known the mind of the Lord, that he may instruct him? But <u>we have the mind of Christ</u>." *(I Corinthians 2:16; Enhanced)*

* * *

"For the wisdom of this world is foolishness with God: for it is written, He taketh the wise in their own craftiness.

And again, The Lord knoweth the thoughts of the wise, that they are vain.

Therefore let no man glory in men: For <u>all things are yours</u>.

Whether Paul, or Apollos, or Cephas, or the world, or Life, or death, or things present, or things to come: <u>all are yours;</u>

And <u>ye are Christ's;</u> and <u>Christ is God's</u>." (I Corinthians 3:19-23; Enhanced)

* * *

"Know ye not that <u>your bodies are the members of Christ</u>? Shall I then take the members of Christ, and make them the members of a harlot? God forbid." (I Corinthians 6:15; Enhanced)

* * *

"<u>Now ye are the Body of Christ, and members in particular.</u>" (I Corinthians 12:27; Enhanced)

* * *

"Now then we are <u>ambassadors for Christ</u>, as though God did beseech you by us: we pray you in Christ's stead, be ye reconciled to God." (II Corinthians 5:20; Enhanced)

***

"Be ye not unequally yoked together with unbelievers: for what fellowship hath <u>righteousness with unrighteousness</u>? And what communion hath <u>light with darkness</u>?

And what concord hath <u>Christ with Belial</u>? Or what part hath he that <u>believeth with an infidel</u>?"
(II Corinthians 6:14-15; Enhanced)

And how many other Scripture verses should we have to quote before it finally begins to sink in?

When Jewish Jesus of Nazareth walked upon this planet Earth, he was the One and *only* anointed individual of God that could truly be called **The Christ**.

However, when God raised up the New Creation Jesus of Nazareth from the dead . . . for every individual that would receive him and place their trust in him . . . God would <u>CLONE *that individual from* **The Christ**</u>, and Xerox them into being the current, active, living, **Christ** among the lost and dying of this world.

***

Jesus of Nazareth did not consider himself to be a sinner because he was not a sinner. How about you? Because, if you do still consider yourself to be a sinner . . . even *a-sinner-saved-by-grace (which in itself is a contradiction in terms)* . . . then you are Biblically incorrect and are not yet *Christ-Minded*.

Jesus of Nazareth did not have to deal with *"old things are passed away"* because there were not any old things for him to be distracted with. How about you? Because, if you are still paying attention to old things such as attitudes, short-comings, various beliefs, erroneous doctrines, or Human divisions... then you are Biblically incorrect and are not yet *Christ-Minded.*

Jesus of Nazareth (functioning as a MAN) did not consider it robbery to be equal with God because he *was* equal by God's own design. *(Psalms 82:6; John 10:34-35)* How about you? Because if you continue to consider it to be robbery... then you are Biblically incorrect and are not yet *Christ-Minded.*

Jesus of Nazareth did not allow the *Realm of the Natural* to dictate their circumstances to him, to try and stop him from what he was directed to do by his loving Heavenly Father. How about you? Because if you allow the circumstances all around you to stop you from what you are directed to do by your loving Heavenly Father... then you are Biblically incorrect and are not yet *Christ-Minded.*

Jesus of Nazareth did not operate under the deluge of circumstances that presented themselves, but rather purposed to rise above all that is seen, heard, tasted, touched, or smelled, in order to see clearly and do what was needed to be done. How about you?

Because, as a *New Creature in Christ* if you are not purposing to rise <u>above</u> all that is screaming in the world around you, and ministering life and light and love to everyone that God brings you to . . . then you are Biblically incorrect and are not yet *Christ-Minded.*

Remember . . . *Christ-Mindedness* is without restrictions, without boundaries, without limitations, without any *Natural* perimeters. **It has already been <u>ESTABLISHED BY FAITH</u>, through Jesus Christ himself, but now is personally <u>ACTIVATED BY BELIEF.</u>**

Because of what Jesus has done, we are now the Supernatural children of a Supernatural God that operates universally in a Supernatural manner and has caused that His Supernatural children are able to imitate Him and in a like manner operate Supernaturally within a Natural world . . . every day. That is what the Mind of Christ will afford us.

However, we must decide whether we are going to focus on the Word of God or upon Television . . . upon the Word of God or upon the Movie Theater . . . upon the Word of God or upon the Sports Arena . . . upon the Word of God or upon the Entertaining Activities that this world offers. It is a <u>must</u> that we renew our minds, and it will not happen automatically by going to church or Bible studies. It has to go beyond that. We must purpose to press-in to the things of Eternal Value. God has done all of the hard work . . . what is our part to play?

CHOSEN GENERATION

CHAPTER 16

*"So all of **the generations** of the Chosen People of God from **Abraham** the first Hebrew, unto King **David** are fourteen generations. And from King **David** until the carrying away of the Chosen People of God into Babylon are fourteen generations. And from the carrying away of the Chosen People of God into Babylon unto The Christ are fourteen generations."*
(Matthew 1:17; Enhanced)

* * *

"But ye are a Chosen Generation, a Royal Priesthood, a Holy Nation, a Peculiar People; that ye should show forth the praises of him who hath called you out of the darkness of Sin and Death, and into his marvelous Light.

Which in time past were not a Called People of God, but are now The Called People of God. Which had not obtained mercy in days-gone-by, but now have obtained mercy." (I Peter 2:9-10; Enhanced)

* * *

"Among whom are ye now <u>The Called</u> of Jesus Christ." (Romans 1:6; Enhanced)

***

"And we know that all things work together for good, to them that love God, to them who are now <u>The Called</u> according to his purpose." (Romans 8:28; Enhanced)

Biblically speaking, a generation of people, *Time-Wise*, is reckoned to be either Forty or Seventy years, depending on the references that are being used to substantiate the expressed point that is trying to be made.

In actuality, Biblically speaking, a generation of people is referring to a specific collection or group of individuals that collectively make up an elite *Calling* predestinatively designed by the Creator of all things.

** **Special Notation:** We are the extremely blessed group of individuals among the specifically designed species of Human-Being . . . that are living within the Preparatory Probationary Period before the unregistered eons of time that lay stretched out before us like wave actions on an open sea.*

The entire focus of the accumulated events within that Preparatory Period of time are designed to establish The Christ (in singularity for foundational purposes) and then invoke duplication of The Christ (en masse) for universal Eternal administrative and governance purposes. It's not really about only the RIGHT NOW, it's about the Everlasting forever ahead as well . . . but since it has to actually begin at some point in time, we can enjoy what God has forever lastingly established within the RIGHT NOW of today!

* * *

Within the Scriptural account we can actually count the generations that are listed by the Spirit of Truth through the Apostle Matthew:

"So all *of* the generations from Abraham to David are fourteen generations.

1.) Abraham 2.) Isaac 3.) Jacob 4.) Judas 5.) Phares 6.) Esrom 7.) Aram 8.) Aminadab 9.) Naasson 10.) Salmon 11.) Boaz 12. Obed 13.) Jesse 14.) David the King

And from David until the carrying away into Babylon are fourteen generations.

1.) Solomon 2.) Roboam 3.) Abia 4.) Asa 5.) Josaphat 6.) Joram 7.) Ozias 8.) Joatham 9.) Achaz 10.) Ezekias 11.) Manasses 12.) Amon 13.) Josias 14.) Jechonias

And from the carrying away into Babylon unto Christ are <u>fourteen generations</u>." *(Matthew 1:17; Enhanced)*

1.) Salathiel 2.) Zorobabel 3.) Abiud 4.) Eliakim 5.) Azor 6.) Sadoc 7.) Achim 8.) Eliud 9.) Eleazar 10.) Matthan 11.) Jacob 12.) Joseph 13.) Jesus 14.) . . . *"ye" in Christ*

"But ye are a Chosen Generation, a Royal Priesthood, a Holy Nation, a Peculiar People; that ye should show forth the praises of him who hath

***called you out of** the **darkness** of Sin and Death, and **into his marvelous light."** (I Peter 2:9; Enhanced)*

As you can see by count, there are 14 generations, and 14 generations, and 13 generations unto, and including, Jewish Jesus of Nazareth. BUT THE RESURRECTION OF CHRIST JESUS FROM THE DEAD CHANGES ALL OF THAT! Because when Jesus is raised up from the Dead he is no longer a Jewish individual . . . he is a new-species of the Human-Being, now known of as a New Creature. And as a New Creature, within the *Predestination* program, he transitions from a singular Jewish individual, into a collective New Creature for all of those Human-Beings that will choose to surrender to the work of the cross, and find their New Life in him! As Jewish Jesus . . . he is the ***"last Adam"*** *(I Corinthians 15:45)*, but within the *Predestination* New Creation program, he is the ***"Second Man."*** *(I Corinthians 15:47; Enhanced)*

We now are collectively known of as ***"the called"*** *(Romans 1:6; 8:28)* and belong to a whole new constituency of new-species Human-Beings. It is imperative that we renew our minds to this new resurrection reality that has been **<u>ESTABLISHED BY FAITH</u>** and begin to **<u>ACTIVATE BY BELIEF</u>** the spiritual realities that now exist because of the work of the cross of Christ. May we choose to fully embrace our New Life in Christ Jesus and ***"put off concerning the former*** *conversation the Old Man* of who we were once, **which is corrupt according to the deceitful lusts; and be renewed in the spirit of our minds** and become transformed; **and that** in addition **we put on the New Man, which after God is created in Righteousness and True Holiness."** *(Ephesians 4:22-24; Enhanced)*

ETERNALLY INDWELT AND EMPOWERED BY THE HOLY SPIRIT

CHAPTER 17

"And I will pray unto the Father, and he shall give unto you another Comforter, that he may abide with you for ever;

Even the Spirit of Truth; whom the spiritually dead world cannot receive, because it physically seeth him not, neither even knoweth of him, but ye know him; for he currently dwelleth with you, and shall soon be dwelling in you for evermore." (John 14:16-17; Enhanced)

* * *

"But if the Holy Spirit of him that raised up the Man Jesus from the spiritual and physical dead dwell in you, he that raised up Christ from the dead shall also quicken your mortal bodies by his Holy Spirit that dwelleth in you Eternally." (Romans 8:11; Enhanced)

* * *

"Know ye not that ye are the very Temple of God, and that the Holy Spirit of God dwelleth in you Eternally?" (I Corinthians 3:16; Enhanced)

***

"That good thing which was committed unto thee keep secure ***by the Holy Ghost which dwelleth in us Eternally."*** *(II Timothy 1:14; Enhanced)*

When Adam was originally created, he had a unique individual spirit, and a soul compliment, and a Terrestrial body *(I Corinthians 15:40)* housing in which to dwell. The Life of God had been imparted unto him, with all transferables, when God breathed into his nostrils. *(Genesis 2:7)* Spiritual Death *(Genesis 2:17)* wrought havoc with the Personage of Man. And God was not going to leave to chance the *Free-Will* volition within the exquisite *Predestination* program participants if His goal for them was Universal management. He would repair the devastation brought about by the power of Sin, and then He promised to personally accompany and walk with the Man, by the Omniscient power of the Holy Spirit, for the remainder of Eternity.

When Man was first created, there was a communication-umbilical that was installed within him, to facilitate creative-clarity from the very heart of God to the heart of the Man. Adam truly had operative *Free Will*, however, the original design, because of the newness of his Being, would function by Adam checking-in with God for direction and possible instruction, rather than simply running off by himself in whatever capacity suited his fancy. That Adam was enamored by having a helpmeet that was a bone of his bones and flesh of his flesh is quite obvious. *(Genesis 2:23)* And when you combine the newness of existence, and the wonder and beauty of creation itself all around you, the very real involvement of authority plus power through personal instruction producing results, and the very influencing factor of twitterpation, you end up with a lethal combination that was tailor-made for the Archenemy of God to assault, utilizing the most subtle of all of the beasts of the field. *(Genesis 3:1)* The Bible tells us that the woman was deceived *(possibly because of lack of information)*, but that the Man was not deceived. *(I Timothy 2:14)*

Whatever the precise details might have been, disobedience caused a communication-umbilical-disconnect, and an immediate two-dimensional darkness brought about denial and shame. *(Genesis 3:7-12)* The rest of the story is Biblical history. God now has to interface with His finest creation through the natural means of the five physical senses because the spiritual road of interior direction and response has been closed. *(I Corinthians 13:12)* God is now on the outside of righteousness-representation and looking in. The Devil, through usurptation now pulls the marionette puppet strings of the Human-Being constituency on the planet Earth. And that condition of two-dimensional darkness prevails for the next four-thousand years until it is *time* to put the *Predestination* Master-Plan into manifested operation.

With the resurrection of the Lord Jesus from both the spiritual and physical dead, repair of Man's perforated spirit can now occur by Divine sealing. *(II Corinthians 1:22; Ephesians 1:13; 4:30)* That is followed by a refilling of the Life of God into that repaired and recreated spirit, *(John 14:16-17; Romans 8:11; I Corinthians 3:16; II Timothy 1:14)* and a pledge of eternal abiding is given, so that a future deviation from the path of righteousness cannot take place. The New Creation Man is now ready for his orientation and training within the arenas of Universal Administration, Maintenance, and Governance.

A promised sweetness of co-habitation with the Holy Spirit of God evokes creative imagination as to what may take place in the eons ahead. Freedom from the threat of Death, in any of its' conditions, is intoxicating. Restored fellowship of loving family and friends virtually lifts the hearts of the participants of this flawless provision.

When training is complete, at the end of the Millennial Reign of Christ, all of the children of the Most High God will report to the Heavenly City New Jerusalem after it's relocation to close proximity to Mankind *(Revelation 21:2-3)*, to accept ownership of their personal mansions. Some children will be returning to the planet Earth for company employment purposes. Some children will remain within the City, at least for a period of time, for unspecified company endeavors. Some children will report to the Executive Office to receive instructions concerning company Governance or Maintenance within the expanse of the Universe. However, all children will retain the Omnipresence provision promise of *"I will never leave thee, nor forsake thee."* (Hebrews 13:5)

Every one of these fantastic New Creation provisions has been *ESTABLISHED BY FAITH* specifically for those who surrender to the finished work of the cross of Christ. All of them shall be *ACTIVATED BY BELIEF* in the not-too-distant future. But why should we wait for something that God has made available for us RIGHT NOW!

BLOOD-RELATED

CHAPTER 18

"Then Jesus said unto them, Verily, verily, I say unto you, Except ye eat the flesh of the Son of man *which is the Word of God*, and drink his blood *which is the force of Life*, ye have no life in you.

Whoso eateth of my flesh, and drinketh of my blood, hath Eternal Life; and I will raise him up at the last day.

For my flesh, *which is the Word of God*, is meat indeed, and my blood, *which is the force of Life*, is drink indeed.

He that eateth my flesh, and drinketh my blood, dwelleth in me, and I in him.

As the living Father hath sent me *to become a Man*, and I live by the Father; so he that eateth of me, even he shall live *Eternally* by me." *(John 6:53-57; Enhanced)*

* * *

"Now therefore ye are no more strangers and foreigners, but fellow citizens with the *other* saints, and of the household of God;

And are built upon the foundation of the apostles and prophets, Jesus Christ himself being the chief cornerstone;

In whom all the building fitly framed together growth unto a holy temple in the Lord:

In whom ye also are builded together with them *for a habitation of God through the* Holy *Spirit."*
(Ephesians 2:19-22; Enhanced)

* * *

"Now the God of peace, that brought forth *again, from the dead, our Lord Jesus, that great shepherd of the sheep, through the blood of the Everlasting Covenant,*

Make you perfect in every good work to do his will, working in you that which is well-pleasing in his sight, through Jesus Christ; to whom be glory for ever and ever. Amen." *(Hebrews 13:20-21; Enhanced)*

Excepting for the shed blood of Christ on the cross, the very subject of blood is given very little consideration. God is smart. And when He purposed to create a moral creature *"in"* His own image and *"after"* His own likeness . . . He knew what He was doing.

The Blood of the Flesh is a physical element, designed by God and Scripturally found only to be connected to HuMan-Beings, is the physical element that God has determined shall carry the very force of Life.

"For the life of the flesh is in the blood: and I have given it to you upon the altar to make an atonement for your souls: for it is the blood that maketh an atonement for the soul." (Leviticus 17:11; Enhanced)

There are three kinds of blood that we find mentioned within the pages of Holy Writ: The Blood of Man *(which is polluted and defiled because of the effects of Sin)*, and the Blood of Animals *(which is not defiled because animals are not moral, and are not held accountable for their actions)*, and the precious Blood of Jesus Christ of Nazareth *(which is not defiled because Jesus did not have a Human father that would pass Sin onto him. [Exodus 20:5; I Kings 15:3])*

Animal blood contains a *repairing element* which is able to effectively cover over, or atone for Sin. That type of blood might be referred to as having *Atoning Life* within it.

The blood of Jesus contains a *remitting and restoring element* which is able to effectively remove or disintegrate any aspect of Sin that it comes into contact with. That type of blood might be referred to as having *Remission Life* within it.

Concerning the origin of Man . . . Adam has no Human father that would pass Sin onto him. *(Exodus 20:5; I Kings 15:3)* And even in like manner . . . as God is the Father of Jesus through the *begetting* process, so God was also the Father of Adam through the *direct creation* process.

* **Special Notation:** *The physical element of blood that ran through the veins of Jesus of Nazareth . . . originally ran through the veins of Adam. When God originally creates Man, He utilizes the Divine Foreknowledge materials that he has prepared for His entire work, including that of Predestination. When He is finished with Adam and Eve, there are no materials left over . . . because they have all been used up. God's utilization of pre-Sin blood to run through the veins of His incarnated Man does not violate any universal laws in any way.*

Adam is the first HuMan-Being that God brings forth . . . and Jesus is the **"last Adam."** *(I Corinthians 15:45)* Adam and Jesus are related by blood even though people do not usually think of that. And because we are descendants of Adam, we are also related to both Adam and to Jesus by blood.

When, after the resurrection of the Lord, the precious sinless blood of Jesus was conveyed to, and placed upon, the Mercy Seat in Heaven, the final chapter was completed concerning the Saga of the Blood. It is still accessible as far as weaponry, but the *Predestination* importance is now fulfilled.

The whole of the program all revolves around Jesus. And he is the one by whom these things have all been ***ESTABLISHED BY FAITH***. You and I are the beneficiaries of these realities, but each and every one of them has been designed to be ***ACTIVATED BY BELIEF***. Purposed focus, renewal of the mind, and dedication will produce the results that we desire. Let is rise up and act, now!

COMPLETE IN HIM

CHAPTER 19

*"**And ye are fully complete in him, which is the** supreme **head of all principality and power."** (Colossians 2:10; Enhanced)*

Complete—*as defined in Webster's Ninth New Collegiate Dictionary:*
1.) To bring to an end and especially into a perfected state
2.) a. To make whole or perfect b.   To mark the end of
3.) To carry out successfully

From the dictionary definition, we can readily see that the word <u>complete</u> means just that... done. However, when we are looking at the application from a Biblical point of view, as in the Scripture verse above, it is referring to the exquisite *Predestination* program. The totality of the needed work has already been done by Christ, and he does not have to do anything else to bring the program to perfection. But we are still the variable within the equation because of our continual resistance to the Truth, and the glitches that we still experience within the arena of our *Free-Will*.

For the most part, we continue to maintain an unrenewed mind. Usually, we do not put on the mind of

Christ even though it has been freely given unto us. We continue to look at, and gauge things, through our natural eye. Circumstances attempt to overwhelm us regularly and distract us from the reality of the Truth.

Jesus has done all of the work, both the difficult and the easy . . . and we need to accept that. Jesus has definitively defeated the power of Sin . . . and we need to accept that. Jesus has made us more than a conqueror . . . and we need to accept that. Jesus has seated us at the right hand of our Father in Heaven . . . and we need to accept that. Jesus has redeemed us from a life of sin and death . . . and we need to accept that. How many times to you hear a Christian say . . . ? *"I'm just a sinner, saved by grace."* That is mostly where our mind is at, is it not? I'm a sinner . . . I'm a sinner . . . I'm a sinner. Do you really think that YOU are a sinner? Do you really want to be a sinner? Do we want to go back to the vomit? Is that why we say things like that? That kind of thinking does not sound COMPLETE to this author.

"But with whom was he grieved *for* **forty years? Was it not with them that had sinned** *through disobedience,* **whose carcasses fell in the wilderness?**

And to whom sware he that they should not enter into his rest, but to them that believed not?

So we see that they *of the children of Israel* **could not enter into** *the promised rest of God* **because of unbelief.**

Let us therefore fear, lest, *an unfulfilled* **promise being left** *unto* **us of entering into his** *prepared* **rest, any of you should seem to come short of it.**

For unto us was the gospel preached, as well as unto them. But the Word *of God,* **preached, did not profit them, not being mixed with faith in them that heard it.**

For we which have believed do enter into *God's prepared* **rest. As he** *previously* **said, As I have sworn in my wrath, if they shall enter into my** *prepared* **rest. Although, the works were** *Predestinatively* **finished from the foundation of the world."** *(Hebrews 3:17 – 4:3; Enhanced)*

* * *

"Let us labor therefore to enter into that rest, lest any man fall after the same example of unbelief." *(Hebrews 4:11)*

Does this not sound like a warning to you? Is the reality of faith mentioned in these verses . . . ? Yes it is. Is the necessity of belief mentioned within these verses . . . ? Yes it is. Have we not continued to declare **<u>ESTABLISHED BY FAITH</u>** and **<u>ACTIVATED BY</u>**

BELIEF in the things that we have been looking at . . . ? yes we have.

We need to choose to believe what God is declaring through His Word, and not believe what our eyes are seeing, or our ears are hearing, or the world around us is saying. We are to become fully persuaded that we are complete *in Christ* RIGHT NOW.

We are Born-Again within our spirit RIGHT NOW . . . We are Recreated after the image of Him, who raised him from the dead RIGHT NOW . . . We are prophetically Incorruptible RIGHT NOW . . . We are resurrected with Christ Jesus RIGHT NOW . . . We are the partakers of God's Divine Nature RIGHT NOW . . . We have been Chosen From Before the Foundation of the World RIGHT NOW . . . We are Supernatural children of the Most High RIGHT NOW . . . We are Redeemed in Christ RIGHT NOW . . . We are the Righteousness of God RIGHT NOW . . . We are More Than a Conqueror RIGHT NOW . . . We are Sin Free RIGHT NOW . . . We are Able To Do All Things through Christ RIGHT NOW . . . We are the fulfillment of Predestination RIGHT NOW . . . We are prophetically Immortal RIGHT NOW and are simply waiting for the new spiritual-bodily upgrade . . . We have the capacity to be Christ Minded RIGHT NOW if we will only press-in to the full persuasion . . . We belong to the Chosen

Generation RIGHT NOW ... We are, even as we speak, Eternally Indwelt and Empowered by the Holy Spirit RIGHT NOW ... We are Blood-Related to the Lord Jesus Christ RIGHT NOW ... We are a Divine Heir of the entire Universe that we live in RIGHT NOW ... We are the Workmanship of God RIGHT NOW ... We belong to the Royal Priesthood RIGHT NOW ... We are Seated at the Right Hand of God RIGHT NOW even as we speak ... We are prophetically set for Administrative duties RIGHT NOW ... And, we are a Household Member of the Most High God RIGHT NOW.

All of these things, and so much more, adds up to the reality that we are Complete in Him RIGHT NOW.

As repetitive as it might get, these realities have all been *ESTABLISHED BY FAITH* even RIGHT NOW. We hold our finger on the button of personal ***ACTIVATION BY BELIEF*** during this present day. May we delay no longer. Be encouraged and grab a hold of that which is already yours ... RIGHT NOW

DIVINE HEIR

CHAPTER 20

*"And if we be **children**, then we are **Heirs**. **Heirs of** the Living **God**, and joint-**Heirs with Christ** Jesus. **If** it so be that we suffer with him as he suffered, that we may be also glorified together with him forevermore."* (Romans 8:17; Enhanced)

A man who is a billionaire is a man who has amassed a great deal of wealth. He potentially has lands and buildings, and stocks and bonds, a great deal of money and chattel property, and possibly even owns towns and cities. Let us assume, for our story's sake, that he has one son and that that one son is his Heir.

Now imagine, just for a moment, that *you* are that one son ... and that your father is a billionaire. What would be going through your mind if that were to be so? How would you talk ... to friends ... to family ... or to men and women in authority? What would you actually do? Would you behave righteously and confidently ... or would you become arrogant and nasty? How would a tremendous amount of wealth actually affect YOU?

The Scripture reveals that we are men and women of incredible position, power, and wealth ... but the truth is that we simply do not believe it. After all, *look, look,*

look . . . the rent is due on Monday, and right now I don't really know where I am going to get the money to pay it. *Look, look, look* . . . other bills are overdue, and unrighteous men and women of the world are exerting pressure on me. Can't you *see?* Can't you *hear?* Are you both deaf *and* blind? Meanwhile . . . the Scripture quietly sits there at the bedside table and declares:

"Now *this* **I say, That the Heir** *of all things***, as long as he is** *behaving and believing like* **a child,** *really* **differeth nothing from a** *common* **servant, though he** *actually* **be** *the* **lord of** *it* **all;**

But *he* **is under** *appointed* **tutors and governors,** *for the sake of instruction and growth,* **until the** *specific* **time appointed of the father."** *(Galatians 4:1-2; Enhanced)*

Remember, <u>***ACTIVATED BY BELIEF.***</u>

"When I was a *young* **child, I spake as a** *young* **child** *would speak***, I understood as a** *young* **child** *would understand***, and I thought as a** *young* **child** *would think***. But when I** *spiritually grew up and* **became a man** *or woman of* **God, I put away** *the* **childish things."** *(I Corinthians 13:11; Enhanced)*

Really, where are we . . . personally . . . on the spiritual growth chart?

Are we so naïve as to think that just because we have reached physical adulthood and we know how to flex our muscles and have sex . . . and have gone to the local public school for x-number of years, and believe that we are intelligent because we keep up with the latest news from the stock market and the political arena, and are knowledgeable of the latest inventions . . . and have asked Jesus to save us from our sins and have gone to the local church in our neighborhood for x-number of years and can quote several Scripture verses, and can hold-our-own during discussions about the Bible . . . that we are spiritually mature and not still a child? Guess again.

* * *

"My people are destroyed for lack of knowledge" *(Hosea 4:6a)* is a current day reality. Not a lack of zealousness, nor a lack of good intentions, nor a lack of Christian *projects* for God, nor a lack of conferences and seminars . . . but a lack of knowledge.

If we do not have the knowledge about God that we need to have, then we really have nothing of value to think upon and to meditate about. Knowledge of worldly ways and worldly things is of very little value within the Eternal scheme of things. We must have knowledge about our God and about what he has done or is going to do. And the religious traditions of men that we are so caught up with and exercise on a regular basis . . . which make *"the Word of God of none effect"* (Matthew 15:6) . . . are more of a liability unto us than they are an asset.

We are not here on this Earth to entertain people with religious jokes and stories, nor are we here to be entertained by others. We are here for a serious purpose. We really should re-evaluate Facebook, U-tube, the Internet, Television and other *life activities* that we feel contribute to our spiritual growth, but in actuality mostly distract us from really hearing from God.

So really, where are we . . . personally . . . on the spiritual growth chart?

* * *

We are already Heirs of God, and inheritors of this entire Universe that our God has created, RIGHT NOW because of what Jesus has done . . . but we have some growth and developmental work to do. The bulk of Christians throughout the world are *immature* and *childish* . . . and in demonstrated denial concerning those issues. And it is imperative that we develop the desire to, and then purpose to, **"put away childish things."** (I Corinthians 13:11)

Realistically speaking, when is it thought that this will happen? When do we personally plan to do something about these issues within our own lives? Will it be right after we finish reading this book . . . or should we put it off for a few more months or years?

The Word of God says that we ***"differeth nothing from a servant,"*** even though we are the lord of it all RIGHT NOW. Do we like getting beat-up by the Devil... is that it? Do we really believe that the Devil is stronger or smarter than we are... Why? Why do we believe such things? Are <u>**any**</u> of these issues that we are touching upon even important to us at all?

* * *

"For where a** Last Will and **Testament is, there must also of necessity be the death of the Testator.

For a** Last Will and **Testament is of force after** the wealthy **men are dead. Otherwise it is of no strength at all while the Testator** still **liveth." *(Hebrews 9:16-17; Enhanced)*

A *Testator* is a particularly specific representative individual, who legally exercises stewardship authority over whatever amount of vast wealth that has been accumulated, and is clearly acknowledged as the one to whom this wealth has legally been entrusted.

An *Heir* is a particularly specific representative individual, who shall legally exercise stewardship authority over the vast amount of wealth that has been accumulated by the *Testator*... being clearly acknowledged and designated as the one unto whom this entrusted authority shall legally pass unto, upon the death of the *Testator*.

The created God-class Man named Adam, was a particularly specific representative individual, who was entrusted with legal stewardship authority, over the accumulated vast wealth of this Universe, by the One and only Living God. *(Genesis 1:28; Psalms 8:3-5; Hebrews 2:8)*

That entrusted stewardship authority, over the accumulated vast wealth of this Universe, was mishandled by Adam and every specific representative individual following him through reproduction, right up until the manifestation of the God-Man named Jesus Christ of Nazareth.

When Jesus of Nazareth, who through Human reproduction became the "last Adam" (I Corinthians 15:45, *and who was also a specific representative individual exercising entrusted stewardship authority over the accumulated vast wealth of this Universe, was murdered . . . there was no Heir for the entrusted stewardship authority to pass unto. He was the last one.*

Upon his resurrection from the spiritual and physical dead, the New Creation Jesus of Nazareth was **appointed** by the One and only Living God to the entrusted position of **"Heir of all things"** *(Hebrews 1:2)*, because there was no one else amongst Mankind that could qualify for that position. And for all of those individuals who have placed their trust in the finished work of Jesus Christ upon the cross, they automatically become **"Heirs of God, and Joint-Heirs with Christ."** *(Romans 8:17)*

We find ourselves in a unique position of entrusted stewardship authority within the world today. But that position is usually not recognized, even though it has been **_ESTABLISHED BY FAITH_** through Jesus Christ our risen Lord. We need to renew our minds to change the way that we think. We need to go beyond the *sight, sound, taste, touch, and smell* of the natural, and press into the Supernatural. Since the results will present themselves as declared by the Word of God when the resurrection realities are **_ACTIVATED BY BELIEF_**, we better get busy and start working on our believing.

WORKMANSHIP OF GOD

CHAPTER 21

*"For we are his workmanship, being **Re**created in Christ Jesus unto good works, which God hath before Predestinatively ordained that we should walk in them."* (Ephesians 2:10; Enhanced)

A typical potter takes the raw clay material from the pit, and by utilizing his workmanship skills, fabricates the embellished vessel of his choosing. It has been stated that "our God is the potter, and we are the clay." This author is able to visualize the Personage of God . . . as a real-life, viable, animated person . . . actively functioning within all of the processes that are needed to bring unto perfection a valued end-product of His workmanship skills.

Contrary to popular thought, we are not merely a constituency of Sin-affected, fallen-from-grace, malfunctioning, free-will, moral beings, caught up and operating within, a willingness of gross immorality, reprobate thinking, and heinous behavior.

We are, in fact, an unprecedented, authoritative, vastly valuable, newly-created creature that the Living God *predestinatively* is molding into actual, genuine, male and female god-members of a Divine Holy Family *(Psalms 82:6;*

John 10:34) that shall exercise supreme dominion and rulership within this Universe, and shall continue on with further inventive endeavors throughout the unending expanse of created *Time*.

"But now hath God set *each of* **the members** *of the Body of Christ* **every one of them into the body,** *according to their giftings and callings* **as it hath pleased him."** *(I Corinthians 12:18; Enhanced)*

Utilizing His unmatched workmanship skills, our God is fabricating the uniqueness of a *predestinatively-*crafted single-entity from a multiplicity of constituents. As we look around, within the undulating walls of Christianity, we see every shape and form of demonstrated Human individuality. First impressions appear to present the awkward idea of a radically-scattering-set of ministerial endeavors much like cockroach-conferences that we find running for cover the moment that the light is turned on. The majority of them pointing to the Heaven above, and shouting CHRIST . . . while resisting genuine Truth in favor of full persuasion, and operating from the Natural beneath, exuding tentacles of jealousy, envy, and self-ishness within established traditions of men in all of its varied manifestations. There is currently far too much of us, and not enough of Jesus living within. Even though it is preached from the pulpit and shouted from the housetops that we are made One . . . there is still far too much of us, and not enough of Jesus living within. The Almighty Self is still on the throne, contrary to all of the righteous protests to the contrary. We are yet fragmented and scattered, and wonderings occur as to when the question will become publically posed... What Is Wrong With This Picture?

It is time for us to get with it, and Get-It. One of the main purposes behind the indwelling **"I will never leave thee, nor forsake thee"** *(Hebrews 13:5)* of the Holy Spirit of God, is the actual process of being **"conformed to the image of his Son, that he might be the firstborn among many brethren"** *(Romans 8:29)* God intends on taking each one of our varying individualities, and intertwining them with the unchangeableness of Jesus, without jeopardizing our unique personality-ness. However, there will be no compulsive-mandate issues coming from Heaven for this to be fully accomplished. We must be willing participants in this process. Now, should there be any validity to that declaration, why are we balking at what the Holy Spirit wants to do, and is painlessly able to accomplish?

The actual thought of being personally caressed by the hand of God in gentile submissive flow alignment is exhilarating. Knowing that He has a perfect plan, and a process to lead me by wooing whispers down a path of correct decisions, with promise fulfilling consequences, is heartwarming.

Our Father in Heaven is the masterful, loving, general contractor of the <u>Body of Christ Project</u>, of which each one of us is an intrigul participant. He is utilizing Foreknowledge-*time* combined with *in Christ* resurrection realities to harmonize into a perfect finished product, free-will, moral creatures destined to become carbon copies of His character and nature.

And all of this has already been **_ESTABLISHED BY FAITH_** and is only awaiting individual agreement and **_ACTIVATION BY BELIEF_** to complete the nuances of a Universe awaiting finished product.

ROYAL PRIESTHOOD

CHAPTER 22

"But ye are a Chosen Generation, a Royal Priesthood, a Holy Nation, a Peculiar People; that ye should show forth the praises of him who hath called you out of the darkness of Sin and Death into his marvelous light." (I Peter 2:9; Enhanced)

And this too shall come to pass.

Any Priesthood, by an understanding of its very nature, is a single individual or a group of individuals that operate in a mediatorial manner, between something or someone greater and something or someone lesser. It is a position of *go-between* if you will.

The origin of Priesthood is to be found in the Book of Genesis in chapter 14 and verse 18.

"And Melchizedek the king of the city of Salem, brought forth bread and wine at the direction of the Lord. And he was the appointed Priest of the Most High God.

And he blessed him, and said, Blessed be Abram of the Most High God, possessor of Heaven and Earth

And blessed be the Most High God, which hath delivered thine enemies into thy hand. And he gave him tithes of all." (Genesis 14:18-20; Enhanced)

There is no Scriptural record of Melchizedek being a part of any already established sect of Priesthood. He is Scripturally seen as a select individual that surely has been chosen and appointed by the Lord of Hosts, who was commissioned to administer a particular blessing unto Abram from God, and the opportunity was taken to establish a provision doctrine for persons that are in a Covenant relationship with the Creator. He was chosen because, at the time, he was the most righteous man upon the face of the Earth. *(The word Melchizedek is not a personal name, rather it is a title meaning "King of Righteousness." The actual name of the individual was Shem, who was the second son of a man named Noah. Shem was approximately 538 years old when he met with Abram, and was seemingly "ageless." His genealogy was not known at that time because he was the oldest individual on the planet, and no one really knew where he came from.* [Hebrews 7:2-3])

* * *

The First occasion of God attempting to establish a collective Priesthood is found in the Book of Exodus when God desires to commission the entire Nation of Israel into a priestly position.

"And Moses went up the mountain unto God, and the Lord called unto him from out of the mountain saying, Thus shall thou say to the house of Jacob, and tell to the children of Israel.

Ye have seen with your eyes what I did unto the Egyptians, and how I bare you on eagle's wings, and brought you unto myself.

Now therefore, if ye will obey my voice indeed, and keep my Covenant, then ye shall be a peculiar treasure unto me above all people; for all of the earth is mine.

And ye shall become unto me a Kingdom of Priests, and a holy nation." (Exodus 19:3-6; Enhanced)

The only nation on the face of the Earth that was in a Covenant relationship with the Living God, at this particular point in time, is the Nation of Israel, which nation God built from the ground up utilizing a man named Abram to establish the foundation. Since God is **"not willing that any should perish, but that all should come to repentance"** (II Peter 3:9) he is going to need someone to be the *go-between* when it comes to informing everyone what the Supreme Master of the entire program desires.

So God declares to His Covenant People, through His spokesman named Moses that He decrees the entire nation to operate as *go-betweens* when it comes to things of Eternal value. Please consider that the Israelites have only recently been liberated from Egyptian bondage. They are currently wandering pilgrims within a natural wilderness. They are not spiritually-minded at all, but rather are focused entirely on the day-to-day issues of survival. Moses, His spokesman, was interested in the ways of God and that which spoke of Everlasting. But the children of Israel were only interested in what they could get from God. *(Psalms 103:7)*

However, that does not alter God or change what He has decreed. God expects more. And the reason that He expects more is because He knows more, and is not going to require something of someone that is unobtainable or not able to be accomplished. So . . . the bar is set, and the children of the Nation of Israel, as a whole, do not live up to what they should.

* * *

Since the entire world seems to be too much for them to handle, God chooses to narrow the margins and the focus shifts onto the Nation of Israel only. This becomes the Second attempt to establish a collective Priesthood among men.

"And, behold, I have given *unto* **the children of** *the Tribe of* **Levi all the tenth in Israel for an inheritance**

for their service which they serve, even the service of the tabernacle of the congregation.

Neither must the other ***children of Israel henceforth come nigh*** unto ***the tabernacle of the congregation, lest they bear sin, and*** they ***die.***

But the Levites shall do the service of the tabernacle of the congregation, and they shall bear their iniquity: it shall be a statute for ever throughout your generations, that among the children of Israel they have no inheritance.

But the tithes of the children of Israel, which they offer as a heave offering unto the Lord, I have given to the Levites to inherit: therefore I have said unto them, Among the children of Israel they shall have no inheritance." *(Numbers 18:21-24; Enhanced)*

The Tribe of Levi was selected to be set apart from the other tribes in the context of *go-betweens*. It is probable that this particular tribe was chosen because of the fact that a man named Moses *(Who is to be utilized as the spokesman of God)* . . . and his brother Aaron *(Who shall be installed into the first High Priest position)* were both from that tribe. Whatever the reason, that tribe was assigned a specific performance of service which involved *mediating* or *going between* God and the other tribes within the Nation of Israel, as well as God and any dealings with the non-Covenant members of the Society of Man.

The Tribe of Levi is the *Priestly Tribe* of the entire Nation of Israel and was involved in all of the services that God ordained including the offering of both gifts and sacrifices for sins. And within the context of what it was designed to do . . . at least for the Nation, it seemed to work well for hundreds and hundreds of years. Additionally, even when the entire Plan of Redemption is complete, the Priesthood activities for the Tribe of Levi shall continue, for the Nation of Israel, forever and ever and ever.

* * *

The whole of the *go-between* Priesthood process was initiated by God utilizing the man named Shem and then formatted into the performance-process utilizing the Nation of Israel. The priesthood is a forever and ever reality process as is substantiated by the established fact that the risen Lord Jesus of Nazareth has been appointed into the Melchizedek High Priest position for a forever and ever allocation of *Time*.

The procurement of a **_called_** constituency of fabricated male and female god-members of the universal ruling-class Family of God is a short 7000-year process. *(Psalms 82:6; John 10:34)* As Christians too many times we do not have a vision for who we are or for the extended future that we are going to be an intrigul part of, but normally only tend to focus on the here and now. God's

Third attempt at establishing Priesthood will ultimately become a resounding success, but currently, it is a dismal failure.

* * *

"But ye are a Chosen Generation, a Royal Priesthood, a Holy Nation, a Peculiar People; that ye should show forth the praises of him who hath called you out of the **darkness** of Sin and Death **into his marvelous light."** *(I Peter 2:9; Enhanced)*

That Chosen Generation of **the Called** *(Romans 1:6; 8:28)* to which we belong . . . that Peculiar People that speak things which be not as though they were *(Romans 4:17)* . . . that Holy *Nation of Righteousness* that Jesus has manifested within his exchange program *(II Corinthians 5:21)* . . . that *third-time-is-the-charm* Royal Priesthood that we are privileged to be a part of *(Romans 12:1; I Peter 2:9)* . . . is what we are talking about, and is what is referenced within the Scripture verse above.

Most of the mystical *Body of Christ* entity, of which we are a member, is made up of previous Gentile individuals. At the outset of the *Body* development process, the majority of participants were Jewish, but that has changed over the centuries that have expired. And regardless of various nuances, we as Gentiles do not come from a background of Priesthood, and really know very little about its operation save what we may have become aware of within a denominationally religious context.

As has been stated previously, the establishment of Priesthood has to do with *mediation*. The First and Second attempts to establish Priesthood, through the Nation of Israel, indeed involved *mediation*, but they were both Foreknowledge-forerunners of the final attempt which, according to the Word of God and the utilization of *The Body of Christ*, will ultimately succeed tremendously. The Scripture tells us that **"there is one God, and one mediator between God and** unredeemed **men, the man Christ Jesus."** *(I Timothy 2:5; Enhanced)* Men, who are currently estranged from God, are in reality at war with God, even if they are unaware of it . . . that is what the word *enmity* actually means. For those men who have been *reconciled* unto God, through the *Mediator* Christ Jesus, they are no longer at war with God. In fact, we become part of *The Mediator* by being members of his *Body*. So, in the commission to go **"into all the world and preach the gospel"** *(Mark 16:15)*, we *mediate* between the Living God, who has literally become our Father, and the members of Humanity that are still at war with Him.

Additionally, within Priesthood activities in these days in which we live, we are to present our bodies as a tangible living sacrifice *(Romans 12:1)*, and verbally offer the sacrifices of praise, thanksgiving, and righteous communications. *(Hebrews 13:15-16)* Very little of this is actually being accomplished.

***

Finally, we are destined to live forever and ever and ever. This planet will eventually reach a population balance with Divine design. When it does the Natural Human-Beings that currently live here, and those future Natural Human-Beings that will continue to be birthed and come forth on a forever and ever basis, will have to plan on colonizing other areas of the Universe when this planet gets full. They will all remain Mortal in their State of Existence and be spiritually-dead in their sins. They will require the leaves and fruit of the Tree of Life to physically sustain them, and they will be in constant need of *mediation* in their dealings with the One and only Living God. Within established Royal Priesthood endeavors we will be the actual *mediators* on the job.

Jesus our Lord ... who is our brother ... has caused these spiritual realities to already become <u>ESTABLISHED BY FAITH</u>. He is the one who will instruct us, by his Holy Spirit, and confirm and commission us to move forward unto accomplishment. The spiritual parameters will never change; however, we shall not have any future difficulty exercising <u>ACTIVATION BY BELIEF.</u> Why don't we purpose to renew our minds and head in that direction RIGHT NOW?

SEATED AT THE RIGHT HAND

CHAPTER 23

"Who is he that condemneth? It is Christ that died, yea rather, that is risen again from the dead, who is even at the right hand of God, who also maketh intercession for us." (Romans 8:34; Enhanced)

"Which he wrought in Christ Jesus when he raised him up from the spiritual and physical dead, and set him at his own right hand, as a Man, in the heavenly places." (Ephesians 1:20; Enhanced)

"If ye then by faith be risen with Christ, seek those things which are above, where Christ sitteth on the right hand of God." (Colossians 3:1; Enhanced)

"Who being the very Brightness of His Glory, and the Express Image of his person, and upholding all things by the word of his power, when he had by himself purged our sins, sat down on the right hand of the Majesty on high." (Hebrews 1:3; Enhanced)

Too many times when we think about God becoming a Man and redeeming us unto New Life through Jesus

Christ . . . in a very general manner many think that God became a Man who was named Jesus, and when Jesus, as a Man, was finished with what he had to do here on this Earth, then he went back into Heaven and became God again. Where do we get such foolish ideas? From bad preaching and Non-Study, that's where.

Each of the Three Persons of the Godhead is God in Their own right. And when one of the Persons of the Godhead became a Man, he was still God at the same time, but he was not functioning as God upon this Earth. And when he completed what he needed to do on this Earth, functioning as a Man, he was still God . . . but he was also still a Man. When he went back into Heaven, he was still God functioning as a Man. And unto this day, and always, he will still be God . . . but forevermore he will still be functioning as a Man.

Jesus Christ of Nazareth was raised up from the dead as a Man. *(God does not need to be raised up from the dead even though He has tasted of Spiritual Death for every Man.)* Jesus Christ of Nazareth was received up into Heaven as a Man. Jesus Christ of Nazareth was seated at the Right-Hand of Majesty on high as a Man. Jesus Christ of Nazareth will forever remain a Man, and will forever function as a Man, even though he is God. Jesus Christ of Nazareth is big-G as God and little-g as a Man . . . at the same time by the exquisiteness of *Predestination*. You and I are designed to function within the forever as little-g Sons and Daughters of our big-G Father. *(Psalms 82:6; John 10:34)*

The highest position that one can hold within the whole of this Universe is that of the Creator. No one sits higher than the Creator. No one has more authority than the Creator. No one will ever trump or override the Creator. However . . . the second highest position that one can hold within the whole of this Universe is that of sitting at the Right-Hand of the Creator. The only one that can trump the second highest position within the whole of this Universe is the highest position which is held by the Creator. Since the highest position Creator and the second highest position Right-Hand seated individuals are in absolute harmony with one another . . . there is no reason for the Creator to ever override the Right-Hand seated individuals.

* * *

When it comes to authority we are talking about who is in charge. We are talking about who it is that gives the orders. We are talking about who it is that makes the final decision. Sadly, most of the time the only two individuals that stand out within any picture of what is going on within our day to day lives is either us . . . or God. And as a Christian, this author cannot tell you how many times that he has heard and continues to hear the statements . . . *"Well, God is in charge." "Well, thank the Lord that*

God is in charge." "Isn't it good to know that God is in charge?" "Well, whatever happens, God is still in charge."

Even though the Word of God says **"and let them have dominion over the fish of the sea, and over the fowl of the air, and over the earth, and over every creeping thing that creepeth upon the earth,"** *(Genesis 1:26)* It is still stated and *believed* by Christians . . . *"Well, God is in charge."*

Even though the Word of God says **"Thou madest him to have dominion over the works of thy hands; thou hast put all things under his feet,"** *(Psalms 8:6)* It is still stated and *believed* by Christians . . . *"Well, thank the Lord that God is in charge."*

Even though the Word of God says **"Thou hast put all things in subjection under his feet. For in that he put all in subjection under him, he left nothing that is not put under him."** *(Hebrews 2:8)* It is still stated and *believed* by Christians . . . *"Well, whatever happens just remember, God is still in charge."*

The Devil, named Satan, usurped the authority that God gave unto Man a long time ago, and utilizing the power of Sin, Satan tricked the Man into *believing* that he was no longer in charge. And even though the resurrection of Jesus Christ of Nazareth soundly defeated the workings of Satan 2000 years ago . . . and has changed everything . . . the Devil is still convincing uneducated, authoritative, Christians that *"Well, God is in charge."* And when a Christian _believes_ that lie, they once again surrender their power and position to a fallen angel. *(Romans 6:16)*

It is no wonder that Christians have as many problems and as much difficulty as they do. They are Scripturally uneducated. They are willfully ignorant. They are blind and are leading others that are blind. Faith and Belief... Faith and Belief... Faith and Belief... they are the two major players in the game. God can give unto us _the_ measure of faith *(Romans 12:3)*, and even tell us how that faith can be increased *(Romans 10:17)*, but He cannot make us *believe,* and He cannot *believe* for us... we have to do something. When will we learn? What is it going to take to make it finally sink in?

Jesus, as a Man, did all that he could do. He walked the path of victory and showed us how to walk that path successfully ourselves. We have been given *Revelation* concerning spiritual truth and reality... but it seems as though we want somebody to do the work that only we can do, for us. Our position and power have been _ESTABLISHED BY FAITH,_ and nothing will alter that. But if we are at all interested in appropriating God's promises and provision, then we must _ACTIVATE BY BELIEF_ that which God has given.

ADMINISTRATIVE

CHAPTER 24

*"And there shall be no night there within the City of New Jerusalem. And they that reside there shall **need no candle, neither** shall they need the **light of the sun; for the Lord God giveth them light.** And they shall **reign** with Christ Jesus **forever and ever."** (Revelation 22:5; Enhanced)*

Within the spectrum of *Operational-Time*, the Scripture verse quoted above is right on the edge of breathlessly awaiting Eons of Eternity. At this particular point, the allocated Second-Probationary Period of Mankind is almost over. *(Romans 9:28)*

The universal rebellion and disobedience that initiated within the Angelic First-Probationary Period of Moral Creation, with a Holy Angel named Lucifer; and proceeded right on through that Angelic Probation and into the entire introductory 7,000 years of Human probation, has been definitively dealt with once and for all.

Lucifer, whose name was changed to Satan to reflect the devastating effect that Sin has had upon him, is incarcerated forevermore within the unending flames of the Lake of Fire. His *little season* *(Revelation 20:3)* is over, and he shall continue to scream at the top of his lungs in pain as the Everlasting years tick by one at a time.

Human *New Creation* men and women spent their first few years in Heaven, following the Rapture of the Church, experiencing a hands-on orientation. All of the *fantasy* bubbles of how they thought that things worked, burst upon their being **"caught up together with them in the clouds, to meet the Lord in the air."** *(I Thessalonians 4:17)* They discovered that the spiritual realities of the resurrection of Jesus, recorded within the immutable counsel of the Word of God proved unaltered, and they began in earnest to learn who they really are *in Christ*. All tears were wiped away at the Bema Seat of Christ as they lamented over how much they had already missed concerning things of Eternal value.

With girded loins they began their ministration of iron-rule enforcement *(Revelation 2:27; 12:5; 19:15)* over the survivors of the Tribulation Period and the Judgment of the Nations events. They have canvassed the Earth and determined who among the current populous is worthy to enter into Eternal Life *(I Corinthians 6:2)* and be able to partake of, and be physically sustained by, the Tree of Life forevermore. They have issued dismissive judgment decrees upon demons, fallen-principalities, powers, the rulers of the darkness of this world, and wicked spirits adversely affecting the heavenlies; and have cleansed the surface of planet Earth of evil entities. *(I Corinthians 6:3)*

The Holy City of *The New Jerusalem* is about to dock within its pre-determined new location above the atmosphere of the planet Earth. God's promise of abiding with men forevermore is being fulfilled right on schedule. *(Revelation 21:2-3)*

The Probationary Period of Mankind winds down to a close as all manifestations of evil, from its inception, are definitively dealt with, and obedience and harmony prevail. The last enemy, which is Death, is finally cast into the Lake of Fire and unintelligent-adverse *Free-Will* decisions will be dealt with swiftly on a one-to-one basis forevermore. No more bulk-probations are scheduled.

* * *

There now exists three separate and distinct *types* of Human-Being creatures within this Universe. Two of them are on a Natural level *(The Jew and the Gentile)*, which shall ultimately become known of as the People of God. *(Revelation 21:3)* And one of them is on a Spiritual level *(The New Creation)*, which shall become known of universally as the Children of the Most High God. *(Revelation 21:7)*

Within the Everlasting that lies ahead, the Universe shall be operated similar to a Family Business. There is the corporation founder of the business *(Which is the God of all Creation)* . . . there is the location of the corporate business offices *(Which is the City of The New Jerusalem)* . . . and there are the corporate employees of the business *(Which in this case are the family members of the Household of God)*.

Business interests and activities shall be the various events and actions that occur within any *Free-Will*, moral Society. We simply extend the parameters of that Society from a planetary level to a universal level. The three basic areas of operations will be Administrative Operations... and Governance Operations... and Maintenance Operations.

Today, with the aid of Hollywood, we can comprehend Outer-Space life-activities, but they are always accompanied with evil, wickedness, hatred, violence, and Death. The concept of those activities is legitimate, but the *darkness* aspect is erroneous concerning future realities. There will be NO evil in active operation. There will be NO wickedness in active operation. There will be NO hatred in active operation. There will be NO violence in active operation. And there will be NO death. And if one of these foul maneuvers begins to rear its ugly head utilizing the gifted, moral, *Free-Will* given by God . . . it will immediately be dealt with in rebellion finality fashion. A swift challenge of the evil shall occur *(Most likely from a Family Member)*, rendering judgment and incarceration into the already existing spiritual prison shall result, for any unrepentant *final-answer* response.

Creativity shall continue on a regular ad-infinitum basis. God originally gave unto His MAN an intellect and a

Free-Will for that purpose. Capacity to speak those things which be not, as though they were, in harmony with gifted creative vision, shall produce what so ever ye desire.

The things that God hath prepared for those who love Him are *off the charts* of our limited visionary thought process of today. But to be sure, the current investment that men and women make, who profess an identification with Christ, shall result in so much more than was ever expected.

These stated truths, found within the record of the Word of God, are all a result of _ESTABLISHMENT BY FAITH_ of the Lord Jesus. Their fulfillment is unalterable and already aligned with Truth. We have an opportunity, RIGHT NOW, to _ACTIVATE BY BELIEF_ the resurrection realities of Christ. To delay is not wise. Make the decision. Start today.

HOUSEHOLD MEMBER

CHAPTER 25

"Now therefore ye are no more strangers and foreigners, but fellow citizens of the Kingdom of God with the saints, and of the established Household of God."
(Ephesians 2:19; Enhanced)

Our closing notation within this little work is one of coming home. The Scriptures inform us that we are **"strangers and pilgrims on the Earth."** *(Hebrews 11:13)* As such, we see people all over the Earth wandering aimlessly about as if they were in a trance. Darkness still prevails greatly within these final Pre-Tribulation years, and one would think that intelligent beings would jump at the chance to miss the destruction and devastation that so clearly appears upon the horizon, even on a natural level.

Human-Beings are a curious breed. Because they were originally created at such an elevated position, they fall prey to the falsehood that they are not a <u>Product</u> of creation *(Even though that Product is propagated by a reproductive process)*, but are actually their own <u>Self-Creator</u>. They readily develop a God-complex concerning their own destiny *(Which they cannot substantiate beyond individual, personal, time-allocation upon this planet)*, and most of the time, choose to factor out of the picture the reality of a genuine Creator. The reality of Physical-Death does not seem to bother them enough to search out Truth, which does not change. Because they have a *Free-Will* they actually choose to *believe* projected lies concerning origins-of-creation, deities-validity, supernatural-manifestations, and unalterable universal-laws, all of which lies and falsehoods have been exposed numerous times ... somehow thinking that an existing Universe is all of a sudden going to alter itself to align with their own comfortable personal *fantasies*.

The Gospel of the Lord Jesus Christ was designed by God to bring individual wanderings and searching to an end. The Gospel is not some sort of Eternal-*fairytale*. The Gospel should not be purported and promoted as being a program that emphasizes shifting from one religion to another religion. The Gospel is a Divine Rescue Plan designed to save those of a *Free Will*, who would prefer not to perish when time runs out. For the men and women who have opted not to perish ... and have become inspired to carry the Gospel forth to whosoever ... the religious emphasis needs to cease and the practicality of Human-Being Rescue from a loving Man, who laid down his life so that the rescue might take place emphasized.

Belief is more deeply entrenched within a Human-Being than *Christians* normally understand. And even though men who once were blind, but now they see are zealous, the reality is that restored Three-Dimensional is not going to be able to talk existing Two-Dimensional into anything. It is only the ***"quick and powerful, and sharper than any two-edged sword"*** *(Hebrews 4:12)* Word of God, that has been provided as the Divine instrument, that shall produce the success that is desired.

Men that are being preached to are not expected to know about the deeper things of God. But the men that are doing the preaching are indeed expected to know. We have been too long wading about in the shallows of Truth. Personal testimonies are nice, but they carry very little real substance. Books of emotional religious emphasis are nice, but they carry very little real substance. Movies about miracles and Heaven are nice, but they carry very little real substance. Deeper knowledge of the Word of God . . . concerning the Personage of God, the creation of God, and the ways of God, are designed to prevail much.

Without deeper knowledge, religious emphasis is what will come forth with Gospel presentation. If there is no validity to that statement, then please present to this author a plausible explanation as to why 2,000 years have expired and this world is deeper into darkness now than ever before. Why is there a two-year time notation within the Scriptures concerning the Revelation teachings of the Apostle Paul and the Asiatic territory that he ministered within? When will we take God seriously?

Coming home is what it is all about. The Personage of God has desired Fatherhood from Before the Beginning. Why create so majestic a creature as MAN if there is going to be no intimacy expected. Master and slave should suffice. Employer and employee will accomplish the task. God and creation . . . pure and simple. However, that is not what the Scriptures hint to, is it? So, why Father and son? Why Father and daughter? Why Family?

During our tenure upon this planet, no matter where we live, we experience the tenderness, and love, and intimacy of Family. All Human-Beings, saving for Adam and Eve, were born, and had parents, and grew up within an influence of Family and friends. Even the most reprobate of men had a childhood and people around them that loved them. It may have been a troubled childhood that is true . . . but they know the longings of "Family" down deep within the depths of their heart. And, so it is also with God.

Too many people see God as having no emotions. He is stoic. He is somber. He is not moved by anything. And, in one aspect that might be true. He does not allow his emotions to govern Him, and to dictate to Him what His next move will be. Unfortunately, men do allow emotions to do just that. God has gone to a great deal of time and expense to build Himself a Family. As the everlasting continues on and on and on it will prove to be well worth the effort that was given. For those that are lost along the way it is a sad commentary . . . but they did have a choice. Now, their names shall be forgotten along with all of the other rebels of the Probations.

The thought of becoming a little g at this point in time is blasphemous and offensive to many *Christians*. They appear to like the idea of false humility. They seem to like the idea of being able to blame it on someone else if what they are involved with does not work. They enjoy being on the lower rung of the ladder. Their vision for Truth is quite limited. But that is not the Plan, and they will soon discover that God plainly said all along what He was going to do within His Word . . . and then He simply went ahead and just did it.

It has been a long, arduous, time-consuming journey that the spirit of Man has taken. Wandering away from home and getting lost. However, our God is patient, and with the resurrection of Jesus of Nazareth from the grip of Death, the porch light was turned on by the Father in heaven, another log was put upon the fire, and a hot cup of cocoa was prepared to welcome the pilgrims back home again. There is no place like home.

Twenty-five Resurrection Realities that are all functioning within the RIGHT NOW whether prophetically or practically. _ESTABLISHED BY FAITH_ and designed to _ACTIVATE BY BELIEF_. Resistance is ultimately futile. A word of counsel

would be to move forward at full steam...do not delay...put the book down and act on what you have just learned. The blessing of the Lord be upon you as you do.

Maranatha!

Meet the Author

By-The-Book Ministries, Inc. began in 2001 as a teaching outreach. Rob E. Daley has been gifted by God to be able to explain biblical truths in an easy to understand manner.

Many have been blessed by his teaching style.

Rob was saved and filled with the Holy Spirit in 1978 and has been instructed by the greatest teacher of all—the Spirit of Truth Himself. Rob is an ordained minister with the Assemblies of God International Fellowship and has pastored in various churches over the past 34 years.

It is the desire of this ministry to see the body of Christ solidly taught, and grow up into the things of the Lord. Rob is available for seminars, retreats, conventions, etc.

Rob can be reached at:

thedaleys@bythebookministries.org

http://robdaleyauthor.com

www.ingramcontent.com/pod-product-compliance
Lightning Source LLC
Chambersburg PA
CBHW020003050426
42450CB00005B/291